From Healing to Whole

A Guide to Root-Cause,
Holistic Healing for Mind, Body & Spirit

By Rachel Van Halteren, R.N.

Copyright © 2024 Rachel Van Halteren

All rights reserved. No part of this publication may be reproduced or transmitted in any form or by any means electronic or mechanical, including photocopy, recording, or any information storage and retrieval system now known or to be invented, without permission in writing from the publisher, except by a reviewer who wishes to quote brief passage in connection with a review written for inclusion in a magazine, newspaper, website or broadcast.

This information is not intended for purposes of self-diagnosis and is not intended to replace the care of a health professional. Seek the advice of a health professional for any health problems you may be having.

Unless otherwise marked, all Scriptures are taken from THE HOLY BIBLE, NEW INTERNATIONAL VERSION®, NIV® Copyright © 1973, 1978, 1984, 2011 by Biblica, Inc.™ Used by permission. All rights reserved worldwide.

Cover Design by Rachel Van Halteren
Revive Press

ISBN: 978-1-0690645-0-9

To my family for all your support, love & prayer.
Thank you for being my greatest encouragers.
A special thank you to my parents for teaching me to think
biblically and to pursue Jesus no matter the cost.

Contents

Preface……………..……………………………..………..9
Introduction…………………………………………...17
Part 1 – The Role of your Identity …………………29
Part 2 – Emotions………………………..……………..51
Part 3 – Don't let Trauma Hold you Hostage………..93
Part 4 – The Physical Sphere of Healing…………...123
Part 5 – The 10 Tenets of Health…………………..137
   Tenet #1 – Water & Hydration…………………..141
   Tenet #2 – Reduce your Toxic Load…..………….144
   Tenet #3 – Sleep……………………………...…...151
   Tenet #4 – Minerals……………………………....161
   Tenet #5 – Nervous System Health……………..163
   Tenet #6 – The Gut……………………………….168
   Tenet #7 – Drainage……………………………...176
   Tenet #8 – Mobility & Strength…………………187
   Tenet #9 – The Quantum Terrain……………….191
   Tenet #10 – Slowing Down……………………...198
Part 6 – Finding Wholeness……………….………..201
Final Words………………………………………….229
Appendix A…………………………………………..231
Appendix B…………………………………………..235
Appendix C…………………………………………..237
Appendix D…………………………………………..239

Preface

Hope deferred makes the heart sick, but a longing fulfilled is a tree of life. – Prov. 13:12

Hello and welcome, Dear Friend!

This book was born out of my own journey to healing. This book is about understanding how God can work wonderful things in you, transforming broken parts, pieces of you that are still in bondage or unhealed, into wholeness and into a fully free, radically beautiful reflection of His image. Our God is in the business of redemption, restoration, healing and freedom. He wants that for you! May this book become your journey to wholeness and healing.

By picking up this book you are stepping into something completely and radically different on your journey to health and healing! I have come to see and believe that a truly unique perspective on health and healing is needed in a world increasingly filled with sickness, suffering and pain. The perspectives and beliefs that I have formed around health and healing have been shaped through many experiences and struggles of my own as I wrestled to find answers and solutions, both as a patient and as a health practitioner.

My perspectives have been shaped by my training and experience as a nurse and natural health practitioner of 15+ years, starting up and running my own health consulting business, the personal rollercoaster of emotions that my own chronic health issues brought me on and the many hours spent in personal prayer relentlessly seeking to discern God's perspective and understanding of health as the Great Physician and Creator of the human body. The countless hours over the many years that I have invested into understanding what it takes to truly heal have been poured into this book. This work is truly special, unique and dear to my heart for many of the reasons listed above. I hope that it will become special for you as you begin working through it and start unravelling the messy journey of healing.

I began writing this book at the beginning of 2024 when I felt God tell me it was time to rest, to take a step back from my business and to focus on letting it all go. It was a step of faith, trusting Him to truly integrate all the time and investments I had poured into my health over the past 14 years. For the first time in my adult life I accepted and received that invitation to rest. That was a big step for me. I enjoy being busy, productive and creative. Stopping has often felt like failure to me, and stepping away from business felt like I was somehow giving up on my dreams. I worried about what others might think.

However, with the grief around the loss of my father two years previously and years of delayed hopes and dreams due to my health struggles, I knew that if I didn't stop and truly attend to my heart, body and soul, all the years of investment would not reap the benefits of what I had sown into around my health and healing. ***There would be a cost to pay if I didn't attend to my whole being – the emotional, mental, spiritual and physical.*** I knew that the time of rest would allow Jesus to do a deeper work of healing. Only He could wrap everything up for me in a neat package, bringing clarity, peace and perspective to my journey towards health. I actually began to get excited, but then felt afraid about 'doing nothing.'

I typically need a creative outlet and I think the Lord graciously gave me the gift of writing as a way to do this and still step back from pursuing health, career, marriage and just about everything else that keeps life busy. The basic concepts of this book had already been floating around in my brain for several months and so I quickly decided that I would begin writing – writing out what was on my heart around health and healing, sharing my own personal healing journey and all the hard and wonderful things that God has brought me through and taught me along the way. My intention in writing was for God to use this process for my own healing, growth and understanding of the journey up to this point…and if He could at the end of it all bless others through what I had written, that would be an incredible bonus!

Since the age of 18 I have struggled with my health in various forms. This was hard for me to accept as an 18-year-old, partly because I had always been strong, healthy and extremely athletic, but mostly because it changed the trajectory of my life in a very short period of time. I had a strong faith but limited emotional skills to cope with such radical life change. Instead of heading to medical school, going overseas to pursue missions, meeting the man of my dreams and starting a family, I spent years struggling with unexplained symptoms and chronic pain, bedridden at times, struggling to perform basic life functions, living on a rollercoaster of emotional frustration and disappointment alternating with optimism and hope. I was in and out of doctor's appointments, visiting with specialists and getting no further clarity as to what was going on or why I was living with random, unexplained symptoms and chronic pain.

Being an optimistic 20-something, I still did my best to pursue a life of some kind of normalcy – travelling, short-term missions trips, job changes, moving provinces and continents, and learning anything and everything I could about health in my pursuit of healing. I couldn't accept that limitation, chronic pain and disappointment were God's plan for my life. I struggled to face my emotions around the delayed dreams and focused my energies entirely on trying the next thing in business or health which helped me focus on the positives instead of how I was feeling.

It is so hard to see what God is doing – or even feel like He is present or cares about you – when you live with crushed dreams from chronic pain or health struggles. It's extremely challenging to realize that specialists have no answers or solutions to your health issues and that you need to forge your own way. I also didn't understand that my emotional distress and habit of shutting down my emotions, my struggles in the area of my personal identity and my unprocessed painful childhood and teenage experiences were contributing to much of the pain I was living with. Those years forced me to draw close to God and rely heavily on Him to get me through each day.

I watched as my peers pursued dream careers, served in international missions, found spouses, had children and bought homes while I bounced from medical appointment to medical appointment, struggling to manage my pain and get through basic day to day function. The sense of aloneness and the intensity of my grief and emotions were overwhelming at times. Yet, God graciously met me there. He grew in me a powerful love for prayer, those hours lying in bed drawing me to my knees, talking to the One who was always there, who never was overwhelmed by my emotions or pain and who was always ready to listen.

Many of you living with chronic illness, unexplained health issues and mental or emotional struggles feel alone. You may have loved ones praying for you and supporting you, which is amazing and wonderful and so necessary, but at some level, it's just you and God. No one is able to step in and change things the way you want or need it to be changed. But God sees you and hears you and knows your heart. Only He can truly comprehend the weight of your struggles and only He can bear the weight of that burden. Most people cannot understand or comprehend the internal struggles or the choices that you make due to your health issues. And honestly, that is okay! I don't think any of you would want a loved one to face what you face.

As I sit back and reflect on how far God has taken me and finally begin to feel an inkling that He is do something good and can make something beautiful with the years that have been stolen, I am humbled and overwhelmed. I am humbled that God stuck through life with me when I was furious with Him that little to nothing I desired or dreamed had happened. I am humbled that He was there when I wanted to give up from pain and disappointment and I couldn't pray. I am humbled that He continued to supply His grace and strength when I was at my end and felt that I'd rather not be here anymore.

I am humbled and overwhelmed by how much He has taught me – about life and developing an eternal perspective in a temporary world, about prayer and the emotional highs and lows of plugging through pain, grief and disappointment, about health and about what it means to truly heal. He has grown in me a resilience that is quite profound, wisdom that only hardship can bring and a compassion with others in their suffering that only Jesus can grow. I'm sure there is much of what I am saying that you can probably relate to!

I want to share *all* that with you through this book. I want you to begin to see and to celebrate God's goodness and love for you, both past and present. I want you to know His deep, unconditional love for you and that He is rooting for you as you seek health and wellness. He has wonderful plans and purpose for your life that you never imagined possible. Physical or emotional or mental pain is not the end of your story. Rather, it is the invitation to an intimate encounter with the person of Jesus, an arrow straight to His heart, because He is familiar with suffering.

When you live with physical or emotional disability or limitations and pain you have His ear. Don't forget that. He is committed to you, to your healing, inwardly and outwardly, in His good timing and way. He *has* brought you far, taught you so much and He will continue to do that. He will carry you when you can't go on and will hold you close when grief or pain seems to be your closest friend.

I want to remind you in the midst of whatever you are wrestling through, that no matter where you are today, no matter how alone or disappointed or angry or sad you feel on your health journey, there is ONE who sees you, who holds you, who loves you, who is always faithful to you and who will always be with you. He can and He will mold you into something beautiful to behold because that is His promise to you. That doesn't mean that the pain will be gone immediately or that the hard emotions will turn into something lovely and joy-filled all the time, but it does mean that you are not alone.

There is hope. There is hope for healing and wholeness.

My prayer is that this book will guide you on a transformative healing journey, equipping you to see your healing more holistically, with a root-cause whole person perspective. If your desire is to be fully healed, then you must begin to work towards health and wellness in every part of who God has made you – the mental, emotional, physical and spiritual – body, mind and spirit, because every part of you requires your attention, compassion and love to truly heal!

Ultimately, my deepest desire is that you encounter Jesus, the Lover of your soul on your healing journey. It is in finding and encountering Jesus, and then being transformed into His breathtaking likeness that you will find true soul rest, whatever the external or physical circumstances you live with. That peace will bring a deep, all-encompassing healing that will radically transform your health, your thoughts, your emotions and your whole being.

Step into this healing journey and anticipate meeting Him and being transformed by Him. He is patient and will be with you every step of the way. And know you are so deeply loved. I have been praying for you!

With love in Christ & in prayerful anticipation of all that God has for you,

Introduction

The Tenacious Pursuit of Healing

*Kind words are like honey - sweet to the soul
and healthy for the body.* – Prov. 16:24

Beginning any journey can initially seem daunting, even more so when it is a journey that you may have taken before and the results were disappointing. The journey to healing can often feel discouraging, overwhelming, lonely, confusing and never-ending. It is filled with highs and lows and ups and downs. Healing is often a lifelong journey since health rarely remains static due to age, life events, injuries, stress and a variety of other reasons or factors. Showing up today to learn how to pursue healing in a new way and desiring to become a better healer of yourself takes courage and determination.

As a health practitioner it is incredibly powerful and inspiring to see the tenacity of my patients and their willingness to grow in their pursuit of healing. When they are ready to reduce their pain, desiring to balance their hormones or to get pregnant, to rid themselves of the constantly swollen or sore belly, or to eliminate the underlying anxiety or the chronic palpitations, nothing will stand in their way and no amount of time, money or energy is too much.

It's truly inspiring to see the hours spent researching health issues, finding and listening to experts in different fields, reading the hundreds (if not thousands) of Instagram health posts, filling the quiet hours with a variety of health information podcasts and spending hundreds of dollars on health products that might get the results they are desperate for.

My training and experience over the past 14 years in the areas of conventional and natural medicine including nutrition, supplementation, homeopathic medicine, quantum biology and more, I often find myself *overwhelmed* by the health information available. At times it can feel that *I* don't know anything, that I don't know enough or I that don't know the right things to help someone heal even in spite of my background and training. I'm certain you can relate to that overwhelming feeling as well, and possibly, the feeling that healing is always just out of your reach.

One of the biggest problems that the average person comes up against in their pursuit of health is finding which 'thing' will bring the most healing. How do you decide which lifestyle change, which diet, or which supplement will be the one that will give you the health you so desire? How do you know which treatment or practitioner is worth in the investment?

To be honest, with access to so much information and a multitude of experts in various fields recommending this treatment or that supplement, the information itself can sometimes be detrimental. In some instances, it can even be a roadblock to your healing. You can be incredibly well informed but also lack the ability to discern what is most effective for *your* concern or issue. This may be because you don't actually know what the real problem is or what is contributing to or causing your symptoms. It could be you lack the funds to invest in specific treatments and/or you don't know which suggestions will provide you with the greatest bang for your buck.

I believe that every person should be equipped to understand the basics of healthcare, the essential pieces that form a foundation to wellness, and how to advocate best for themselves when facing sickness and disease. Sadly, our educational system hasn't prepared the majority of us to do this. In addition, too many of us have been hurt, dismissed or medicated excessively by a well-meaning, but poorly equipped and undereducated healthcare system, particularly when it comes to a more natural and holistic approach.

My desire in this book is to help you become an effective navigator of health information and to help *you* become the best guide and expert on your health journey in the most *efficient*, *effective* way. Wasting time, energy and money when you heal is not fun. And let's be honest, who has time for that?"

This guide will not miraculously transform you into a doctor or natural health professional. However, you will learn to become an expert in yourself: someone who truly understands you. You will begin to acquire the skill of listening to your body's unique voice, paying attention to it's needs, triggers, traumas, responses and how to respond in ways that bring health, healing and hope (because we all need a little hope on this journey!). I will teach you to ask yourself the hard questions that need to be asked for healing to occur at a root level. I will empower you to think differently about how health and wellness are accomplished and help you learn skills that will provide a holistic perspective to your healing.

This approach to healing is a process and it may initially seem unclear why you need to work through areas of your being that may have never been addressed before as part of your physical, emotional or mental health treatment provision. I would encourage you to hang in there and trust the process as many of the questions and exercises that I walk you through will empower you to heal more effectively. In fact, many of the questions that you will be asked may need to be reviewed over and over again as you peel back layers of disease from years of underlying and contributing factors to your current health situation.

Don't give up hope though! The more familiar and proficient you become with the process, the questions and the healing exercises, the more you will give your body what it needs to heal as the changes create a foundation of wellness in your body.

Is our Healthcare System Truly a System of Care?

Health and healing have been overcomplicated by making it into a 'system' of care where we have been told that the doctor knows best. We need a return to a more personally empowered, self-taught experience of health. In no way am I saying that some of these approaches or supplements, medications or treatments are invalid, unhelpful or not required at times, but health is a personal experience with personalized needs. Sadly, in a system of healthcare, the individual needs of the person get lost because personalized healthcare is expensive and time-consuming. Particularly since COVID, we are experiencing a healthcare system that is overburdened and unable to deal with an increasingly ill population. You *need* to become better at healthcare for yourself to thrive.

The seeming complexity of our healthcare system has made illness or disease appear to be a localized or specific body system issue requiring a specialist in a specific field of medicine. For example, a mental health issue is often labelled as a chemical imbalance in the brain requiring medication that will correct this imbalance and treatment by a psychiatrist. An autoimmune issue is defined as dysregulation in the immune system needing treatment by a rheumatologist and medications that suppress the immune system from overacting. In reality, both mental health issues and autoimmune diseases can have deep roots in the emotional, mental, spiritual and physical sphere that require a holistic approach!

Although these might be oversimplified examples, our healthcare system rarely looks at the whole person and fails to address the disequilibrium within the mental, emotional or spiritual areas which could be contributing to the development of these problems in the first place. In doing so, it will fail to bring true, root-cause healing every single time. When you consider that the word 'disease' truly pays homage to the idea that there is dis-ease (or disequilibrium) within the body, it is a good reminder that we need to delve into some of the places that are often ignored in our pursuit of healing and health.

The tools for health and healing are also a lot simpler and within your reach than you have been led to believe. The oversimplicity of these healing approaches may be exactly what makes people seek health in more expensive or ineffective ways, such as in taking vast numbers of supplements and incorporating complicated diets and lifestyle changes to their healing regimen. These can be helpful at times, but healing does not necessarily or always require this level of cost and energy. Healing treatments for some of the most complicated diseases really are right around you and accessible in the form of the natural world and delving into the way we think, feel and experience life.

There is a time and place for investing in working with a natural or holistic health practitioner because they have invested incredible amounts of time, energy and money into an education that is devoted to helping people heal naturally. Don't dismiss the medical specialist who is invested in your health just because you've been shamed for your symptoms or you've never had a medical doctor help you heal or truly let you give voice to your experience.

A mistake I often see people make in the healing journey is doing it completely on their own. Yes! Learn from the blogs, the podcasts and the online gurus because they will help you to ask better questions and advocate for your needs. However, inviting an expert into your process can save you a lot of time, energy and money as they can give you specialized direction for the next step in your journey having seen 100s if not 1000s of patients. Their training and real-life, hands-on experience cannot compare to yours, in spite of your hours spent researching.

That all being said, I want to encourage you and help you in this journey. I don't think you need to spend astronomical hours or dollars you don't have to get the results you need. Yes, healing can be extremely complicated and sometimes very expensive, but I believe that what most people need is a proficient, knowledgeable guide.

You need a health coach that can give you the foundational elements to good health, who can ask you the questions that need to be asked as part of your healing journey and who will listen to your specific requirements and concerns. You need someone who can save you time, hours and give you a shortcut to the best health information. You need someone who will help you acquire a different perspective on your health and think more holistically so that you can truly heal. *That person is you.*

Before you get overly concerned that I'm setting you up for failure or that you feel the task is too overwhelming or that your health journey has already been long and complicated and becoming your own coach is daunting, let me ask you the following questions. Who knows *you* best? Who is the most reliable at listening to your body's unique voice and needs? Who has the most valuable insight into your specific traumas, triggers and personal history? The answer to at least one (if not all!) of these questions is, or will be, you!

If you are willing to invest some time, energy and effort in become an expert in yourself, not only will this book guide you through developing the skills necessary to learn a holistic approach to healing but you will become a better coach, self-advocate and carer for your own needs. Becoming connected to yourself and fully aware of the amazing complexity of what makes you unique will empower you and enable you to pursue healing in a deeper, holistic way. The goal of this book is to set you up for success in your healing journey.

The beauty of developing these skills will not only save you time, money and effort, but it will also help you become cognizant of when you may need external support from expert practitioners or how to advocate for what you feel is necessary for healing in the next steps of your journey. Healing is such a fluid experience, shifting from season to season and life event to life event, that your improved self-awareness and self-care will be an invaluable tool in knowing what is your next best step. My greatest desire is that this workbook provides you with the absolute fundamentals to a successful healing journey.

The healing tenets I share later in this book form the foundation to health regardless of the health issue or symptoms you deal with. They are simple, affordable and reliably give incredible results. They may seem a little 'out-there' or too simple to you initially, but I'm asking you to have patience and a little faith.

Many of you have been exposed to a lifetime of approaches to health and healing that are based more on societal trends and a general ideology around health that is limited and consistently has rejected alternative approaches to health and healing. You may have to reverse a lot of lies and uncover long-held beliefs about health that are completely contrary to what you grew up believing. However, the fact that you are here, reading this book means that you are already questioning the way health is pursued and you are open to a new way of thinking! Congratulations!

By implementing the Healing Tenets in Part 5 and working through the Healing Questions and Healing Exercises in this book you will benefit and begin healing at a deeper level that may not be immediately obvious or give you the results you want to see straight away. Remind yourself when you don't feel or see the changes you desire immediately that health is an investment. The outcomes take time and are cumulative. Don't be fooled into believing that quick results are the answer. You are learning to lay a wonderful groundwork and nutritive soil for healing that will benefit you long-term and provide a foundation that will increase the benefits of whatever treatments you do when you do need to work with a health practitioner.

Kickstart your Healing with…

To start you off on your healing journey I want to state that the most foundational piece for good health and for healing is this: you need to slow down, start paying attention and begin having a lot of compassion with yourself. In a society that values quick results, quick solutions and the biggest bang for your buck, it is vital to remember the best investment into your health and healing is time, attention and self-compassion, which sadly are often the resources we lack the most.

We live in a society that is extremely busy and we are often extremely self-critical, lack self-awareness and are impatient with ourselves and the process of healing. *This will have to change* as you pursue true holistic, root-cause healing. With this in mind, you will notice that the majority of this book will take you on a learning journey of attending to yourself in every sphere: mentally, emotionally, physically and spiritually.

Paying attention, slowing down and developing self-compassion are <u>fundamental</u> to health and healing. You won't know how to heal if you don't know what to heal, or if something is actually working or if certain things are contributing to symptoms. You need to take the time to slow down which in turn gives you the ability to focus on yourself and your needs. Healing occurs best when you create space and time so you can make choices that are necessary for healing to occur.

The most foundational piece for good health and for healing is this: you need to slow down, start paying attention and begin having a lot of compassion with yourself.

Healing requires rest in a way that is not just stopping because you are in pain. It is a complete slowing down mentally, physically and emotionally. It is a putting aside of the pushing and the striving so that you can truly rest. It might mean letting go of the outcome or goal you had so your body doesn't feel under a constant sense of pressure and stress. It may mean learning new ways of being with yourself that are kinder and more compassionate. You cannot heal when you don't have time or space to acknowledge problems or learn healthier ways of being.

Health is a journey. To this day, in our conventional medical system we've been fed the lie that health is a quick fix. Honestly, we often want the easiest and quickest solution. I get that. I want that for you too. So, let's make the steps you take the *most* effective, the *most* powerful, the *most* healing. Each step you take and every decision you make, physically, spiritually, mentally and emotionally, will feed into the fruit of your labours for health.

This guide is about reframing the way you see yourself, your health, and your ability to exert any type of control over health.

Remember that *health is cumulative* and sadly, most of us have accumulated a lifetime of emotional garbage, physical and mental trauma, and poor lifestyle choices related to our nutrition, sleep and mobility. Today begins your chance to begin the undoing of all of these, the first step on a cumulative health journey that will empower you to make changes that will benefit you today, tomorrow and in a few decades. Will it take discipline? Yes. Will it involve some life changes? Yes! The fact that you've already picked up this book shows that you are ready and willing!

Finally on a last, but no less important note: You may be tempted to skip past various sections of this workbook to get to the 'good' stuff (usually related to what you can *do*, and that which avoids the emotions, the pain of trauma and anything that feels uncomfortable). However, don't underestimate the role that the emotional work plays in healing the physical body.

When I began my own healing journey, I initially only addressed the emotions and traumas that I couldn't avoid. It took a lot longer for me to see and experience the beauty of the effort, time and space needed in the uncovering of and working through the past hurts and traumas which seemed to have no relevance in my current health situation. However, I can tell you that the emotional work around my experience of emotions, past trauma, the way I would talk to or think about myself, attitudes around my identity and how I worked through my emotions were just as important in the physical healing process as the physical changes I implemented.

Healing takes time and it is a process. You will find yourself jumping into one part of this book and then stepping away from other things because you don't have capacity in that moment or because something triggered you to deal with it. See triggers as invitations by your body to do healing work in those areas. View your symptoms as your body's way of speaking and not as the enemy to be shut down and suppressed. Slow down and pay attention to the unique way your body speaks – because it is unique to you! Without you paying attention to your body's needs and desires you are in actuality fighting yourself and limiting the healing that could be available to you.

You cannot heal fully without a holistic approach.

Healing is like peeling layers off an onion. It's one layer by one layer. Each layer may call for a new approach, a different supplement or a unique therapy. This workbook isn't a linear process just as healing isn't linear. Feel free to jump around as you integrate new disciplines, new patterns and new mindsets. Allow yourself to slow down, to *feel*. Feel what is comfortable, what is uncomfortable and ask the questions why. Be gracious when you can't do something and need to choose something else to focus on. You can always come back to it later.

This process is unique to you and it is yours and yours alone. However, you aren't alone in this process either! You have a faithful Father God who is your Healer and Friend on this journey with you. At times you may feel alone, shipwrecked, raw, vulnerable, angry, sad, furious, irritable, hopeless, happy, celebratory and host of many other emotions. Allow yourself to go there, acknowledge and feel. Don't bottle it up. Express your pains, thoughts, emotions and fears to God because He cares and He knows and He holds you wherever you might be with whatever you are feeling and experiencing. If you don't yet know how to do that, do not fear! You will learn!

Remember that there is nothing Jesus cannot relate to, no mountain too big for Him to traverse with you, no pain that He cannot handle. And as you journey through, you will delightfully and surprisingly find yourself on the other side of that mountain, not quite knowing how you arrived there in one piece, possibly a bit battered and bruised, but still whole, still human, but OH!, so much more capable, resilient, fulfilled, healed and with a new perspective that changes the way you see yourself, your health, your life and your future. Let's get started!

Slow down and pay attention to the unique way your body speaks – because it is unique to you! Without you paying attention to your body's needs and desires you are fighting yourself and limiting the healing that could be available to you.

Part 1

The Role of your Identity in your Healing

I praise you because I am fearfully and wonderfully made; your works are wonderful – Psalm 139:14

You are here today, working through this book with the goal of healing your body, your *self* to the fullest and in the most complete way possible. In order to do so, we need to start with discussion about the self, *yourself*. Now, I don't want you to get the wrong idea here or feel that you're about to entertain a 'me-first,' self-centered cultural ideology. No! This discussion around your identity is not a secular or worldly view of the self, nor is it about making everything about yourself. Rather, it is about understanding and uncovering a realistic view of who you are as a human being created by God.

This is a conversation and a deep dive into your *identity*. This is about your value and your worth because you are a child of the Creator King of Heaven, a co-heir with Christ, a person created by God with a specific purpose. Even if you are reading through this book and do not believe in God or Jesus, this is a reminder that you are loved by God and have beautiful worth and inherent value because you are a human being, uniquely you and created by God!

Although it may seem a little odd to begin a book on healing with a chapter on the self and identity, I can honestly say that, having worked with many clients and having done a lot of healing myself (yes, for physical health issues!), **how you view yourself is central to every sphere of health: the mental, physical, emotional and spiritual.**

The connection between these four spheres of yourself form a crucial foundation to health and healing yourself physically. Neglecting any of these areas will impact your healing journey, possibly delay healing and even prevent full healing from occurring. You need to understand *who you are* and *who you were created to be* to live out your greatest potential, to heal and to thrive. When you are in pursuit of real root-cause, holistic healing you must address every part of yourself as much as you are able.

The mental, emotional, physical and spiritual parts of yourself are constantly interacting with each other and have influence on each other. Therefore, restoring health to each sphere is an essential piece of this healing puzzle. When one area is out of balance it affects the health of the other areas.

I'm sure you have seen or experienced how your physical health profoundly impacts your mood (think of those days you deal with pain and the havoc it wreaks on your energy, your ability to interact with others, your ability to give and receive), and so it is that your mood and emotions can influence your physical health. In fact, your gut health (the physical sphere) is commonly called your 'second brain,' influencing your body's ability to make neurotransmitters which in turn shape your mood (your emotional and mental sphere). This is why you are starting with the basics: the truth of *who you are* because *you* are the one in need of healing!

When it comes to identity and healing you need to understand yourself, how you view or see yourself, and how you talk about or to yourself both in your mind or out loud. Having a negative or untrue perception of yourself, whether it is expressed through word, thought or action has definitive consequences for your emotional, mental and physical health.

Proverbs 18:21 says that 'The tongue has the power of life and death.' This verse is not just speaking about the words you speak to others; it includes how you speak to and about yourself! When you do not speak positive, truthful and life-giving words and truth to one area of your being, you deny health to yourself as a whole.

The Power of a Word

Science has shown the power of words on the health of living things. In fact, speaking kindly to a plant improves its growth! How much more do the words we speak to ourselves impact our ability to heal and to thrive! We've all heard how one negative word spoken to a child has significant power to undermine confidence and self-esteem even to the point that it can affect the potential of that child all the way into adulthood. This is due to the release of stress hormones in the brain when negative words are repeatedly spoken, putting the body into a chronic stress response and ultimately altering the stress responses at a genetic level. These physiological changes to our childhood brains from these words have far-reaching power, even to the point that one is more likely to develop autoimmune diseases, mental or emotional disorders and other chronic illness later in adulthood. Words can shape your mental, physical and emotional health and resiliency for the rest of your life or until you work through the emotional trauma of those words.

When you do not speak positive, truthful and life-giving words and truth to one area of your being, you deny health to yourself as a whole.

It takes many more positive words to undo the power of one negative word. The truth is that this doesn't change as you age. As such, many of you reading this book may be in a state of reduced stress resilience stemming from words you or others spoke to or over yourself in childhood. The repetition of those negative or untrue words within your own minds to this very day continue to feed this state of being, affecting your personal identity and prevent deep healing from occurring. Negative words can continue to reinforce false identities that feed into your emotional, physical and mental health.

Unfortunately, we experience additional negative verbal reinforcement from the world we live in, engaging with a culture that is extremely self- and other- critical which only serves to compound the power of negative words in our lives. We are told that we should be in better physical shape, that we need Botox or plastic surgery to look 10 years younger and that we should wear the latest trends (and look good in them too!). We are bombarded by photos and expectations that are unrealistic and are tearing our self-image into pieces.

Society tells us to define our value and worth by what we can do, our career, what we accomplish, how much success we have, how much money we make, how fertile we are, how productive our days have been, how happy we look on Instagram, how we feel and a million other shallow life markers and standards. We will never meet the standards of the world but we continue to let those standards influence our perception of ourselves and our value.

The lies we believe about ourselves may stem from words spoken over us as children or they may be from the constant exposure to unrealistic standards on social media. They may even have been formed by living with the on-going experience of disappointed hopes and dreams due to the experience of living within a body that can't, hasn't and doesn't live up to our needs, wants or expectations. Therefore, it becomes an imperative part of our healing to expose the lies we've believed about ourselves and to stop feeding the critical monster that tells us we are and will never be enough.

Who Will Have the Final Say?

To begin our healing, we must come face to face with our value system. When we realign our value system to God's Word it frees us up to redefine our worth using His standards: the inherent worth that God put into the essence of our being at conception and even before we existed! We have Kingdom value and worth because our Creator says it is so. He made us and He knows what our potential is even with the limitations He has allowed in our lives at any given moment.

It is essential to start to speak *His* truth over our lives, which in turn will have life-giving power over our emotional, mental, spiritual and physical health. The way we think and talk about ourselves needs to be recalibrated by God, who made us and knows our value, worth and potential because He made us! We need His view of ourselves to become our only view of ourselves from this day onward.

You have Kingdom value and worth because your Creator says so.

When we find our identity in our actions, in what we accomplish, in our appearance or what the world states as valuable or worthy, we will always be working to try fulfill or prove. A Christ-centered identity brings us into a place of rest. There is no need to prove or strive. There is no need to compare. In fact, we will never fall short in our value when we accept His words about our true value and worth.

Learning to rest and be is a hard but necessary step in your healing. The being and resting in our God-given value feeds into a sense of freedom and peace that is not of this world and which has far-reaching threads into our physical, mental and emotional wellbeing. It's even more powerful when we consider that an identity in Christ doesn't change.

The way you think and talk about yourself needs to be recalibrated by God, who made you and knows your value.

He gave us value regardless of circumstances, health situations, diagnoses, productivity levels, financial records, marital status and many other worldly expectations and standards. When we find our identity in Christ, we can let it all go and rest in the arms of the One who made us. Our mind can come to a place of stillness and we can abide in Him. That's a place where healing occurs. That's a place that brings life.

Throughout my adult years I struggled to hold a full-time job (or even sometimes work at all) due to my physical health issues. My mom repeatedly told me that my identity and value were not defined by the world's standards but by God's standards. She reminded me that the things that I was capable of doing given my physical limits, such as being available for my family, investing in my siblings lives spiritually and emotionally, and spending time praying, were the most important work - Kingdom work!

However, I felt these things were small and insignificant and I continued to hold the world's standard because what I could accomplish felt of little value and fell far short of the goals and dreams of what *I* wanted from my life. I felt like I was a constant disappointment, a physical and financial burden on my family and that my value was somehow less because I 'contributed' less. I was disappointed with my body as I wrestled to function physically on a daily basis.

My mom's reminders were helpful but the lie that I was somehow 'less-than' others or not enough because of my physical limitations was a constant and powerful thread running through my mind that held greater power over me than the truth of God's identity and purpose for me. The lies I spoke over myself so frequently, particularly on days when I was dealing with more pain or physical limitation, had more power than those gentle reminders. The repetition of these lies in my mind and aloud became the bedrock on which I built my life on and they became my reality and truth. In the few instances I did speak God's truth about who I was I had a hard time believing them because the lies were deeply embedded.

As I have worked toward physical healing, I have come to a Spirit-led awareness that my identity is fundamentally linked to my physical health. When I am hard on or highly critical of myself and speak lies about my value, feeding into thoughts of failure, disappointment and sickness, I create more stress on myself and my body pays the ugly cost of slower healing, increased symptoms and more inflammation. When I tell myself I am 'too much' or that I shouldn't feel a certain way, effectively shutting down the sensitive and hurting parts of myself, I am rejecting parts of myself and ultimately how God made me. He created me with a sensitivity to other's feelings, compassionate and with a whole plethora of emotions. These beautiful parts of myself can easily and quickly become areas of shame that continue to feed into sickness of the soul, mind and body.

When I take a step back and look at what my body, mind and spirit has been capable of, has done and overcome in spite of the injuries, the pain, the sleepless nights, the hormone imbalances, the mental, spiritual and emotional struggles, to name just a few things, I realize that I have developed incredible resiliency that I rarely acknowledge or celebrate.

I am still learning to stop myself from reverting to 'fix-it' mode where I relentlessly try to figure out what I did wrong to cause the flareup. I am slowly realizing that the unrelenting pressure I put on myself and holding to the standards of the world are detrimental to my health. More than that, it isn't what God created me for. I am learning to appreciate how God has wired me as a person, rather than fighting against His design of me and for my life. I have come far, grown in wisdom and compassion, and have developed an understanding for others because of my struggles.

Have you ever stepped back and observed your life objectively or had someone reflect your life and your experiences and triumphs back to you? Do you ever speak true, honest words of appreciation for the strength your body, mind and spirit have? Have you ever celebrated how your body has enabled you to go for a walk, show up to work, give a friend a listening ear, knit a scarf, cook a meal or carry a baby? Do you speak words of life, encouragement, joy and healing over yourself regularly or are your go-to words ones of despair, disappointment or hatred?

This is often a challenging area when you live with chronic health issues, whether they be mental, physical or emotional. Living with them can be an emotional, physical and spiritual rollercoaster, never knowing what new symptom or struggle you will wake up to. The highs and lows of inconsistent health can completely throw your emotional state and your daily plans out of balance. It becomes too easy to speak words over or to ourselves that reek of disappointment, anger and frustration.

Don't get me wrong! Emotional honesty is great! Being honest with ourselves and with God about those struggles is invaluable and necessary. However, it is in moments like these that there is opportunity for healing words, self-affirming words and hopeful words. These words have power to shift your perspective and align your mind, body and spirit with the One who holds in you those hard moments.

Healing involves creating new rhythms of behaviour, thought and speech around yourself and your health. Can you move from 'fix-it' mode or problem-solving mode into a place of rest when your body or mind is not where you need it to be? Can you remind yourself that your identity and value is not defined by your current struggles but by a loving Father who knows you better than you know yourself? Yes, you can and you must acknowledge the pain or disappointment that accompany the journey to healing because it's important to be aware and feel our emotions and have compassion with ourselves. However, remember that your words have power and the ability to give you life.

You *can* declare healing over your body. Start by declaring truths about who you are and your value as a child of God. You can claim promises of God's purposes to give you abundant life, joy and peace in the Holy Spirit and His strength that is not of this world. Create life-giving potential for yourself by regularly celebrating who you are and how far you have come. Celebrate how much wisdom and compassion you've learned through all your health struggles and all the traumas and pain you've experienced in your past.

Letting God Define & Re-define You

God's perspective and a solid knowledge of who you are as His child is the only perspective that truly matters. Your health does not define who you are or your value to this world. It may impact what you can physically do or even emotionally handle, and that's okay! You are not the all-powerful God and you don't need to be perfect or capable of handling everything or rescuing every family member or friend in need. That's God's job. It's in your weaknesses and limitations and struggles that God's strength is exhibited and you learn to lean on Him more, allowing Him to fulfill your needs and the needs of your friends and loved ones.

I find myself closest to God in my suffering and struggles even if I'm terribly upset with Him that day because I'm wrestling with my health, my purpose or with disappointed hopes. Living with my physical and emotional limitations and challenges, I am faced with the daily reminder that I live for another Kingdom: God's eternal Kingdom. I am reminded that my prayers have power and that the times of flareups and forced rests are invitations to spend time with Him. He's jealous for my time and attention. Those prayers and forced rest times have greater power and more value than any million-dollar paycheck.

My worth is defined by *who* I am and not what I do. My identity cannot be in the things I can or cannot do because every day may bring a new symptom affecting my abilities. Living with an identity that is defined by what the world deems valuable means that I will always fall short and I will always be disappointed with myself. That is a heavy burden to bear and isn't meant for a child of God. His burden is light. Part of your healing is about surrendering the process and the outcome of the healing journey and trusting that God has you exactly where you are supposed to be in any given moment or situation.

You matter to Him and so your health matters to Him. He is a Healer God and He is with you on this journey. Commit your way of healing to Him and He will guide your steps (Prov. 3:5-6). His goodness and mercy follow you all the days of your life (Psalm 23) even when you don't feel great. Remember God is in your process and He is God *of* your process.

God has you exactly where you are supposed to be in any given moment or situation.

The days when you are physically, emotionally or mentally limited by your health are days of opportunity to rest in Him. They are opportunities to speak with Him about your purpose and ask Him about your identity. The days of forced rest create opportunity to evaluate how we view ourselves and talk about ourselves.

God created you in His image, with an identity that is special and unique to you. He knitted you together in your mother's womb, knows every word before it's on your tongue and works in every situation for your good. He has plans and a future for you. He is abundant Life and He has given that abundant life to you. His desire is freedom for you!

Learn to daily declare these truths and other truths from scripture over yourself, especially when you are feeling down and discouraged about your health. Speaking the truths of Scripture such as, 'God is working in these circumstances for my good,' 'He loves me,' and 'He is my Healer, my Defender, my Strength and My Deliverer,' give life, hope and courage to the heart that is failing or feeling hopeless. Remind yourself regularly that He loves you, that He is for you and that He sees you. Prophetically declare healing over yourself because His desire for you is healing and wholeness. This declaration is an act of faith that you believe God's design and intention for you is health and healing and that you stand aligned with the truth that He is able to do it!

You need to start creating patterns of behaviour and thought that are lifegiving and nourishing to your body. How encouraging it is to your body when you speak a healing, kind word to an ailing body (and spirit!)! They are essential to it's healing potential and repair! **These words will come more naturally when we know who we are and when we have aligned our minds to His truths as a regular discipline.** Not only do these words bring life and healing to your body, mind and soul, but they are fundamental in changing the neurological pathways in your brain so that you don't live in a state of constant stress.

Repeating these life-giving words can permanently change the way you think bringing more robust emotional, spiritual and mental health! There is a reason that psychology and counselling encourage the use of 'positive affirmations' as part of therapy. They work. How much more will the truths of Scripture bring life, peace, joy, hope and healing!

As you pursue a deeper understanding of your value and worth in Christ and as you seek to understand your God-given identity, I want to challenge you to move from the truths of Scripture and into a deeper relationship with your Maker. He wants to spend time with you. He wants to speak to you about how much He loves you. As He is the God who speaks, the Living Word, you can expect Him to show up to meet with you.

He wants you to ask Him about your unique identity as His Child. He wants you to know who you are fully, personally and as His uniquely loved child. He wants you to live out your God-given identity, a place that is filled with joy and life-giving purpose and perspective. It may take days or weeks of time with Him to hear those words but I promise He will show up because that is what He does. He shows up and He speaks words of life and identity over you. He wants you to know those words, to be defined by them and to live them out.

I want you to give them some serious thought as you enter into the Healing Questions section. Take a few days or weeks to answer them, mull over them, and get some clarity about them. Get into the Word of God and read His truths about who you are. Pray and ask God to speak His truth of who you are to you. If you have a trusted friend, spouse or mentor who loves you, knows you well and who you can trust, ask them to share their insight and perspective into yourself, because to be honest, we aren't always the best judges of ourselves and we *need* an accurate picture to begin healing at the deepest soul level. There may be a divide between what you see about yourself and what is actually true – and time, repetition, prayer, repentance may all be part of the healing of that divide. But it can happen! If I can do it, you can too! It is never too late.

Speaking life to our bodies is essential to healing and needs to be a discipline that is practiced regularly. Words speak life so start speaking life today!

Healing Questions Part 1:

1. What were your gut reactions to the ideas brought forward in this chapter? Freely jot down any thoughts or feelings that came up while reading this chapter.

2. Think about how you speak about or to yourself (in your head, out loud, to others, when you make a mistake, when you are unwell or experience another flare up of symptoms, etc.)? What are some common things you say about yourself both positive and negative? Write them all down.

3. Write a truth from God's word or perspective responding to *each* of the negative words or phrases that you wrote about yourself in question #2. Speak these truths aloud over yourself.

4. Write down a list of your strengths (example: resilient, resourceful, faithful, loyal…etc.). Take a moment and celebrate those!

5. If you have someone you trust and who loves you ask them if they could share:
   a. What they love about you?

   b. What they see are your greatest strengths or giftings?

6. On a scale of 1 to 10 (1 is no confidence, 10 is extremely confident) how confident do you feel about yourself – physically? Emotionally? Mentally? In your decision-making?

   a. For the areas where your score is 5 or less, take some time to consider and write down what limits your confidence or has fed into these feelings?

   b. What are some words that you could speak that are true about yourself and would build your confidence physically? Mentally? Emotionally? In your decision-making?

7. How do you think others perceive you?

a. Do other's opinions about you concern you more than God's or your own?

8. How do you think God sees you?

9. There are may verses in the Bible that speak about your identity. Take some time to look up the following Bible verses that speak about your identity and right down anything that really strikes you and why. There are many other verses so have some fun googling other verses around your identity in Christ.

- You are made in God's image. (Gen 1:27)
- You are fearfully and wonderfully made. (Ps. 139:14)
- You are the apple of God's eye. (Ps. 17:8)
- He delights over you. (Zeph. 3:17)
- God has plans and a future for you. (Jer. 29:11)
- You are child of God. (1 John 3:1)
- God takes pleasure in you. (Ps. 147:11)

10. Are there truths about who God says you are that don't line up with the way you talk or think about yourself? Take some time using the prayer written below to confess each of these out loud to God now.

> Prayer of Confession: Father, I have believed __(name the lie)__ about myself. It is not true. I renounce this lie in Jesus' name and repent for believing this about myself.
> I speak the words of (read the bible verse or truth that corrects this lie) and speak these as truth over myself. I thank you that you have given me a new identity and ask that would continue working out a new understanding of my identity in You. In Jesus' name. Amen

11. As you worked through this chapter what emotions come up for you as you learned more about your identity and its connection to your health?

    a. How did you respond to those feelings?

b. Where in your body did you feel those feelings?

12. Based on the above questions, was there anything you learned about yourself? Take a moment to celebrate and thank God for how He has made you! Tell yourself you are proud of you because you did the work and can see your strengths and your value. You are beautiful wherever you are in this process of uncovering your identity in Christ! Praise God for the beauty of His creation – you!

Further Resources on Identity

I have listed a few additional resources that might be of help to you if you wish to spend more time exploring your God-given identity. God wants you to know and walk in your God-given identity. He created you with unique potential and unique purpose. The resources I have shared below are helpful for teaching you to uncover lies you have believed about yourself and uncovering God's words of identity that He has for you.

Resources:

Winship, J. (2022). *Living Fearless: Exchanging the Lies of the World for the Liberating Truth of God*. Revell.

Benner, D. G. (2015). *The Gift of Being Yourself: The Sacred Call to Self-Discovery*. (Expanded ed.). Intervarsity Press.

Identity Exchange. (n.d.). https://www.identityexchange.com/

Part 2

Emotions: Connecting the Heart & the Body

A peaceful heart leads to a healthy body; jealousy is like cancer in the bones. - Prov. 14:30

Good ole' emotions. Their presence is like the air you breathe, always with you, flowing through you, playing an intrinsic role in your life. They come in a variety of shapes, sizes and colours. However, what you do with them, how you engage with them and how you feel about them is a whole other factor. You may love them, hate them or just 'put up' with them. You may label them as positive or negative, ultimately doing whatever you can to avoid the negative and embrace only the positive. You may have learned to express your emotions or to ignore them or shut them down. Sometimes they just come out of nowhere and take you by surprise. There are moments when an outburst will bite you in the butt.

Maybe you feel that logic and reason are better than emotion and that emotions are the 'enemy to reason.' It's possible that you live your life out of your emotions, making every decision based on how you are feeling in any given moment. At times your emotions feel like an embarrassing younger sibling that you've had to make excuses for your whole life. It's possible that you've stuffed emotions so deep down that you don't even know how you feel or what anger feels like or how to cry anymore. Wherever you are with your emotions, however they currently feel or don't feel, I want to tell you that that is okay.

Emotions are an integral part of you. God created you with emotions and they play an invaluable role in your life, allowing you a glimpse into how you are doing in any given moment or situation, affecting how you respond or react and how you think in different situations. You can't escape or eliminate your emotions because they are how God designed you in order to truly experience a full and abundant life.

You can't escape or eliminate your emotions because they are how God designed you in order to truly experience a full and abundant life.

When you consider how intense emotions can feel it is no surprise that they have energy that can be measured – through heart rate, blood pressure, facial expressions, body language and more. They have a unique energy of their own; for example, the heaviness or sluggishness of depression or the rush and vivacity of joy. These energy-filled emotions are meant to be experienced and then released, like swimming through a wave on the ocean, feeling and engaging with them without judgment and then letting them pass along by, as you move through different situations and life events.

In discussion with older generations around the subject of emotions and emotional health, there has been a level of discomfort expressed around this topic; in fact, emotions were often considered a private thing for you to deal with on your own. The reality of this approach was that a lot of emotional expression was seen as embarrassing to self and others and as such it was shut down or ignored. Today we live in a society that is much more interested in having conversations around emotional awareness, expression and health. Many of you would agree that that is a positive thing.

On the other hand, we have swung so far in the other direction that our emotions and feelings have become the truth by which many people live. Life-altering decisions are made purely on an emotion or feeling that lacks any foundation in truth and reality. Decisions made this way often result in very poor outcomes mentally, physically, emotionally and spiritually. We are in desperate need of a healthy understanding of emotion, of ways of expressing emotion and of living in a space that allows our emotion, reason and Biblical principles to play a combined action in the decisions we make.

Many of us today are trying to find the right balance when it comes to feeling and expressing emotions in our daily lives. Growing up in our different family environments and though our life experiences, we've picked up emotional habits and patterns, many of which have not been beneficial to ourselves or to others. Unfortunately, personal investment in emotional health has not been given as much attention as it needs and so we were often left on our own when it came to learning how to deal with our emotions.

As we enter adulthood, we begin to realize that our lack of emotional skills has had negative consequences on our relationships, our communication abilities and our life choices. We may have hidden shame or guilt related to this area of our life and this is holding us in further bondage and preventing us from doing more healing. Not only that, but as we become more aware that our emotional health and resiliency have a direct impact on our physical and psychological health, we continue to lack the support we need to learn and develop our skills in this area.

Learning to Connect the Dots Between the Emotional & Physical Sphere

My experience with emotions as a child may sound familiar or somewhat familiar to many of you - I grew up shutting my emotions down, feeling terribly embarrassed if I cried, defining emotions as 'negative' or 'positive', and ultimately thinking emotions were the enemy that had to be ruled by logic and reason. I avoided or ignored the negative emotions (a main reason why I don't like labelling them as such) which meant that I either suppressed, repressed or held onto them by, not recognizing that emotions were not my enemy.

I didn't understand that if I engaged with the 'negative' emotions, feeling them and having compassion with myself rather than judging them, they would simply pass on and I would be all the happier for it. Entering into adulthood, I soon realized that I couldn't just 'get rid of' my negative emotions and they would, at some point, result in an emotional 'blow up,' or they would find some other way of getting voiced. It took me over 26 years to begin to see that many of the emotions that I suppressed or ignored, either due to my own discomfort with them or because my family environment demanded it, found their voice in the physical pain and other symptoms I was living with.

Even beginning a healthcare career, I never considered the tremendous impact and entanglement of emotional health on physical health. In fact, it was the furthest thing from my mind. Nursing education taught an ideology that disease, illness and symptoms were the result of poor lifestyle choices, genetics, and biology. You just inherited 'bad genes' or you made poor lifestyle decisions which eventually affected your health. Treatment was whatever drugs were prescribed and if you found a more 'progressive' doctor there might be some discussion around the food you ate and an encouragement to be more physically active. Emotional health was rarely, if ever, part of the healing equation, unless there was a diagnosable mental or emotional disorder.

When I started to develop more serious health issues at age twenty-three, I knew that the healthcare system's pharmaceutical approach to treatment was something that I wanted to avoid due to the side effects. Like many of you, I began this healing journey on my own, researching and addressing my nutrition and ingesting as many supplements as possible to support my health. These more natural approaches provided some relief but it was often short-lived and the investment was financially steep and time consuming. A single dietary 'error' would cause my symptoms to flare up again.

In spite of the time, money and energy I put into my health I was always in some state of flareup and pain. Even though I felt more "in control" and happy that I was treating my symptoms naturally, I wanted more healing than the small amount I was experiencing. I truly believed that God had made the body with greater capacity to heal and that there had to be a way to get more permanent and deeper results.

As I delved further into natural healing approaches I took an introductory course in homeopathic medicine. The philosophy of this medicine turned my understanding of health and healing upside-down and made inexplicable sense to me. This was hard to accept as a student of western medicine, where homeopathic medicine was often equated with quackery and lacked the scientific evidence that would deem it as a valuable and viable treatment option. I remember sitting in my first homeopathic consultation as a student and thinking how unusual it was that we were asking in-depth questions about a person's emotions, emotional experiences and past traumas as part of a health consultation. Never before had any medical consultation I was a part of took this into consideration!

As my homeopathic education and training continued, I could not deny that this holistic approach made sense and that the results were somewhat miraculous: People with significant illness and disease were improving when the whole person was being addressed and treated! I began to see connections and patterns between the development of a disease or illness and a person's personality, emotional health and expression, their history of personal trauma, recent or chronic stressors and particularly from profoundly life impacting events even as far back as childhood. All of these non-biological factors impacted the onset of disease and the appearance and reappearance of symptoms or disease! It was mind blowing!

Recognizing the connection between the physical and emotional is not the same thing as being equipped to deal with this phenomenon I was observing in my patients. I had so many questions because my nursing education and upbringing had formed in me a perspective and understanding of health that didn't encapsulate the whole person as part of healing.

How could emotions so significantly impact the body that disease would result? Did this mean that healing was more than just a biochemical experience? Could it be possible that there was some inexplicable phenomenon that science had not yet uncovered? How did one start to treat the emotional part when medicines and treatments were purely physical in nature?

One thing I knew was that results don't lie: addressing emotional health and past emotional experiences as part of a health treatment brought about positive outcomes that could not be denied or dismissed as pure placebo. Experientially I was being challenged to accept that there was another way of healing that had something to do with emotional health and expression and history of suppression of emotion and life trauma.

Uncovering the Role of Emotions in Illness

Today, the role of emotional health in physical healing isn't as 'out-there' a concept, but it was definitely considered such 10+ years ago. Mainstream medicine had begun to talk about some associations between certain emotions and physical symptoms, particularly in the areas of anxiety and its host of symptoms or the link between chronic stress and the development of stomach ulcers. However, the investment into understanding and treating the far-reaching impact of emotional stress and emotional trauma was not a consistent part of routine medical practice. Education in the health field did not address the role of emotions and past trauma on health let alone talk about integrating regular emotional health check-ins as part of medical treatment.

As you work towards health and wellness you want the medicines and the treatments you undergo to do the majority of the healing work. That makes sense! You put your health and lives into the hands of experts who should understand how to help people heal. You have invested time, money and energy into various modalities and treatments that were prescribed, natural or otherwise. You may be getting fairly consistent results from these therapies or treatments and it may even maintain the level of health you currently live with. That was also my experience.

However, it wasn't until I hit roadblocks to healing or when treatments stopped working or being as effective that I really started to accept that a more holistic view of was going to be necessary. I started making those connections between my own emotions and my physical symptoms. I began to start asking myself some hard questions around the cost of pursuing healing.

Would working through childhood, teenage and adult experiences that had fed into my emotional patterns be worth the cost? Could I truly begin to set better emotional boundaries if I wanted healing? Was I willing to explore painful past experiences that cemented my attitude around my emotions? Would it be worth it to develop more emotional skills and build resiliency in this area for greater health? This meant that I had to take full ownership of my need to do emotional work. It meant that I would have to be uncomfortable emotionally for a time.

I decided that my health was worth it. I wanted more healing. I wanted to be free – free from patterns that were damaging my health and feeding into long-term dis-ease in my body. As I stepped into a healing journey in this area I began to see more permanent change in my symptoms and flareups. Deeper healing was beginning to occur!

Delving into your emotional health and personal history feels uncomfortable, inconvenient and unrelated to the physical part of your health because that is what our health system has led us to believe. However, if you are like me and you want more healing than what you are getting from the investments you have made into your physical health, it is time to come to a deeper understanding of the role of your emotions on your unexplained symptoms, your chronic illness and your mental and emotional state.

Pray for wisdom and understanding as you face this truth and begin to take steps to implement changes. Your body, in spite of the physical care, treatments and all your investment, might be stuck in a constant hyperactive, reactive state stemming from the way you live your life: living in a state of unmanaged chronic stress, shutting down emotions or just not dealing with them well and not acknowledging or dealing with the pain of past trauma. This reactive or sympathetic state puts you at a disadvantage, weakening your overall health physically and reducing the efficacy of the treatments and therapies you are investing in.

The Power of Emotions in Dis-ease

As we explore this area further, we need to understand more about the influential role of emotions on our physical body. Our lack of understanding of the relationship between our physical and psychological health has a far-reaching impact that must be addressed or it will continue to wreak havoc on your body unbeknownst to you. Emotions are powerful things and have incredible ability to create dis-ease or disharmony in the body if not attended to.

Positive emotions, like joy or hope, are lifegiving and nourishing to your body at a cellular level, while 'negative' emotions, such as anger or bitterness or jealousy can be more destructive to the body. To be very clear here, I want to emphasize that the 'negative' emotions become destructive to the body when they are held onto long-term or if they are repeatedly suppressed, repressed or ignored.

When those 'negative' emotions are suppressed, ignored or held onto they can actually get stuck in the physical body (particularly the fascia), upsetting its delicate biochemistry and patterns of communication within the nervous system, the digestive system, the circulatory system and more. This contributes to dis-ease.

When you think about how many of us today are living in a state of chronic stress, have unmanaged or suppressed emotions, trauma and unhealthy emotional patterns, it is unsurprising that many people have trouble healing their bodies. Your body requires a state of calm and safety, also known as a parasympathetic state, to heal and benefit from whatever treatments you invest in.

The chronic state of stress from these factors and the resulting disequilibrium of the body may initially show up in emotional burn-out, anxious, feeling chronically or easily emotionally drained, overburdened and even the sensation of feeling physically heavy. These feelings contribute to high levels of physical tension and stiffness which can increase and promote physical pain. You may develop systemic inflammation and find yourself increasingly fatigued. You may find yourself in a state of over-reactivity or oversensitivity to the slightest triggers, physically, emotionally and mentally.

Your body requires a state of calm and safety, also known as a parasympathetic state, to heal and benefit from whatever treatments you invest in.

Although your body has incredible capacity to respond to stress and adapt to the emotional baggage you carry, your body will not hesitate to rewire the body-brain connection into the sympathetic state. This state does provide a semblance of protection, but it is a survival state built for short-term success and not long-term balance and health.

The body in distress will make its voice heard if you do not attend to or you ignore its needs for too long or too frequently. Suppressed or ignored emotional pain and trauma *will* find a way of voicing itself, inhabiting parts of your body and showing up in those symptoms that make no sense. It will appear as emotional or mental symptoms. Over time, it will develop into chronic disease or dysfunction.

> *The body in distress will make its voice heard if you do not attend to or you ignore its needs for too long or too frequently.*

To more fully understand what a body in a chronically dysregulated state looks like, let's explore some symptoms. I want to point out here that these symptoms are chronic – usually present with regularity for a minimum of 3 months and can persist for years. They become a part of your 'normal' although they are not in any way normal and they do not feel good. These chronic symptoms can show up on their own or with other symptoms, varying from day to day or week to week. So, what are some of the symptoms of a chronically dysregulated state?

They may include symptoms such as an elevated or irregular heart rate, anxiety or agitation, feeling 'off' or on edge, feeling frozen or stuck, shortness of breath, nausea, stomach pain, irritable bowel (diarrhea, constipation or some combination of the two), constantly feeling overwhelmed or overstimulated, irritability, sweating, easily being startled, hypervigilance and more.

Other symptoms that may be part of this chronically dysregulated or stressed-out state which are often left out or unrecognized include a) difficulty healing despite high levels of investment, time and energy and/or b) the onset of an illness, disease, mental or emotional disorder or other unexplained symptoms after experiencing a chronically stressful or traumatic childhood, trauma, chronic stress or a significant life-altering event.

Our poor emotional health, lack of emotional skills and inability to handle stress and trauma can result in the development of dis-ease any time in childhood, the teenage years and as adults. These, in combination with our life experiences, can affect our brain chemistry, significantly rewiring it to a chronic stress state.

Your nervous system can also become dysregulated through personal experience of adverse childhood events or multiple traumas throughout childhood and adulthood. This nervous system dysregulation is then compounded by our lack of emotional skills and/or our ignorance of the role emotional health plays in our neuropsychology and physical health as adults. We need to learn skills in the emotional and psychological arenas that can retrain our brains to be in a calmer, more relaxed parasympathetic state to begin healing many chronic illnesses, symptoms and mental/emotional disorders.

Lastly, it is important to address one more insidious factor that may be contributing to your health issues. This is the *inherited* stress response. In fact, many of us are unaware that we show up to our lives already having been dealt a hand that makes us less resilient to stress, more susceptible to dis-ease and more reactive to what may be easily manageable triggers due to our *mother's* emotional health and experiences of trauma during her pregnancy and post-partum phase. These factors play a role in your physical health, resiliency and stress response in childhood all the way into adulthood. Consider then how powerful the combination of both maternal and personal emotional dysregulation and how that can wreak havoc on your health, setting the stage for future dis-ease.

Who Actually Cares for Your Emotional Needs?

As we turn to professional help to heal in today's world we face a lot of challenges. Culturally in North America we have been heavily influenced to think that our healing and health is vitally connected to medication, conventional doctors or different types of medical treatments. We think of health and healing as a biochemical experience requiring biochemical treatment in the form of pharmaceuticals, surgeries removing injured or diseased tissues and other aggressive treatments on our bodies. Sadly, this approach is limited and inadequate as health issues and dis-ease stem from so many other factors.

Removing a dis-eased organ or tissue or taking a pharmaceutical in cases of chronic disease does not typically treat the root of the problem in the first place. In fact, it can push dis-ease deeper into the body creating more pathology or sickness. An example of this would be the suppression of childhood eczema with the use of corticosteroid creams and the development of asthma later in life.[1]

Another example that illustrates why addressing the deeper issues is important to healing is the link between childhood trauma and autoimmune diagnosis in adulthood. When you consider that 25% of those diagnosed with an autoimmune disease develop additional autoimmune disorders,[2] you can begin to see that it's important to go deeper into what might be contributing to dis-ease so that health is not further compromised as you age.

The scientific literature also shows a link between adult chronic depression and unprocessed childhood trauma[3] and heart disease and chronic depression.[4] Although these studies may be observational in nature and science cannot directly correlate emotions with disease, this does not negate the link between the two. The reality is that our bodies are not just physical beings. We are also emotional and spiritual beings that live in a physical body. There is no separating the influence that every sphere has on each part.

This is why addressing root-cause problems, such as emotional trauma, becomes an essential part of healing. Even with increasing awareness of the link between our emotional and physical health, our medical system still does not integrate a more holistic treatment approach since medical professionals are typically equipped only to work within the physical realm of dis-ease.

Even though we may assume a more holistic approach in the natural medicine world, it too can be very disjointed when it comes to the actual treatment of every part of our person in the treatment of health problems. It's usually the counsellor or therapist that addresses the emotional issues and the naturopath, acupuncturist, or physiotherapist that addresses the physical health issues. It is the Pastor or Spiritual Director that will help through the spiritual struggles.

Although I logically understand this approach as people work within their skillset, I also feel that leaving these spheres to the different professionals is one of the reasons why healing takes so long and why more healing does not occur. How often are you encouraged to see a therapist by your physiotherapist when the physiotherapist sees there might be an emotional link to the physical pain? Or to see a Pastor by your Naturopath?

We need someone to tell us that it is *essential* to address every aspect of our being to pursue healing and routinely ask, as part of our treatment plan, if and how we are doing the work in *each* sphere. We often judge conventional medicine for its fragmented approach to health but the reality is that in natural medicine we don't approach it much differently. We might acknowledge the link but natural health professionals typically don't integrate this holistic approach into treatment or we just assume patients will pursue holistic help on their own. Patients rarely pursue a fully holistic approach and it does more unintended harm than good.

Emotional Healing: Where Do You Begin?

In order for real, root-cause physical healing to occur, particularly for chronic disease, unexplained symptoms and mental or emotional disorders, the healthier you need to become emotionally. You must learn *how* to become emotionally healthier. You were created with emotions and you experience them every day of your life in every situation. They impact the decisions you make and affect your relationships regardless of your opinion on them or how healthy you are emotionally.

So, what do you do with your emotions? How do you learn to allow yourself to truly feel your emotions and what role do they play in your healing? How do you learn to express emotions well and understand where they 'fit in' as part of your daily life? How do you deal with emotions long-buried or emotions that are brought up from past pain and childhood trauma?

To begin with, I want to remind you of the most important truth about this journey: ***God is committed to your healing.*** We aren't left completely on our own, without any guide as we uncover past hurts, learn new ways of being or develop healthier skills. As Christians we have the Word of God to provide fundamental and life-giving truth to our emotional experience. We have the Holy Spirit within us who can comfort us, guide us into what is true, help us live out lives that overflow with the fruit of the Spirit. Love, joy, peace, patience, kindness, goodness, faithfulness, gentleness and self-control are not out of reach! In fact, they are part of your inheritance as a child of God and are being worked out in you as you surrender your daily life, struggles and celebrations to God.

It may be that you grew up in a church or a Christian home where emotions were dealt with in ways that were detrimental or affected you negatively. Statements such as, 'you should just align your thoughts to God's Word' or 'speak truth over yourself,' might have been a common approach to dealing with hard or negative emotions. You may have been told that emotions such as anxiety, anger or sadness were sinful and therefore you ignored them, suppressed them or felt shame for feeling them.

If we fall into the pattern of not working through these emotions and telling ourselves that we should not or are not supposed to feel anxious or angry, we are ignoring a large part of the beauty of how God created us. Responses such as these do greater damage to the redemption possible for our emotional being. God created us with emotions because they have a purpose: they can be helpful indicators that something is right, wrong, unjust, painful or needs to be addressed. They play an essential role in living out a life filled with the fruit of the Spirit and help us live out the abundant life that we are promised when we walk as children of God. Our emotions are just as much a part of our reflection of God's image as our rational thoughts. They too were influenced by the effects of sin and as such also need redemption. As such, they cannot and must not be ignored.

You may feel overwhelmed by the fact that you need to invest in another area for physical healing to occur. Yet, you are a child of God and His promise is that He works in all things and in every situation, using them for your good (Rom. 8:28). He is not taken by surprise by the home you grew up in, the traumas you experienced, the health you are currently living with or your level of emotional skills and resilience. His commitment is to make you healthier and whole in every area of your being. He wants to break off shame and bring freedom to where we are in bondage. We were not left adrift in this world or left on our own to figure out how to pursue wholeness in the area of our emotional health. There is hope for healing and for growth in the area of our emotional care and wellness.

Although emotional healing will look different for you than it does for me, the principles are the same. It is time to acknowledge that you have emotions, that they impact you and that there is room to grow! Emotional healing begins with developing emotional self-awareness, learning how to experience and feel your emotions, learning how to express your emotions from moment to moment in healthy ways, building emotional skills, growing in self-compassion and possibly doing the opposite of everything you may have been taught from childhood!

His commitment is to make you healthier and whole in every area of your being.

In your journey to emotional health, you will also discover that it isn't enough just to feel and deal with your *current* emotions; you will have to work through patterns developed from all the pent up, 'stuck' emotions that you learned all the way back from childhood or other past traumatic events. This will not happen overnight. This can sound overwhelming and impossible, but I want to encourage you that even though it may feel that way and the journey may seem arduous, it is work that is vital to wellness and will bring great reward and even greater freedom!

Part of your healing journey is acceptance and grace with where you are at today in this moment. It's learning to be compassionate with yourself but also coming to understand that there comes a day (maybe today!) that you will need to learn a new skill, a better and more life-giving way to deal with the emotions you experience. Growth starts small, with the tiniest seed, with a little water and sunshine.

This workbook is here to help you become aware, learn some simple skills and practice them so that you can have a healthier future. Even if you it seems overwhelming or too difficult to see or identify what specific emotions are contributing to your symptoms in this very moment, your willingness and ability are so incredibly valuable.

Learn to slow down, begin to pay attention to yourself and learn your body's unique voice as expressed through your symptoms. Your ability to acknowledge that the experiences of your past and the emotional or physical effects of those experiences on your body and mind is a stepping into your healing. Don't criticize the small beginnings.

Lastly, let's acknowledge the other elephant in the room: another aspect contributing to our failure to work through the emotional pieces of our health is that at some deep, subconscious level we probably don't really want to get into the nitty gritty uncomfortable work of dealing with our emotions and past trauma. Dealing with emotional health is uncomfortable and painful work at times and it often feels worse before it gets better. It can seem like there is little purpose in addressing this area because we aren't as familiar with working on improving and healing emotional trauma as part of the physical healing journey which has made it seem as if it doesn't play a fundamental role in physical wellness.

The emotional pieces, past and present, may feel unrelated to your current circumstances or symptoms and at times we feel that they are best left untouched. We need to get better at making the healing of every part of ourselves accessible even if we are just peeling back the top layer and going about it extremely slowly. My hope for you in this section on emotional health is that it opens up a door of exploration and ignites curiosity as to how your emotional health and patterns are impacting your current level of health and your ability to heal.

Grief as a Part of Your Healing

There are two aspects of the emotional healing journey that I would like to discuss in further detail before you begin working through this section's Healing Questions. The first is that grieving plays an immense role in your healing and is often forgotten or overlooked. A measure of healing comes when you finally acknowledged and truly allow yourself to feel the sadness of loss and pain due to poor health, the lost years, the delayed goals, the giving up of dreams and hopes and the on-going disappointments from a life impacted by chronic health issues.

I pushed through many years of poor health with a very optimistic attitude, striving for the day when I would finally, hopefully be fully healed. This meant I often ignored or only gave partial voice or expression to the painful sadness I felt from the delayed dreams and disappointed hopes along the way. I was too busy hoping for a future that wasn't guaranteed and instead ignored my sadness and pain.

My lack of emotional honesty with myself around these hindrances contributed to my poor health as inner stress and disappointment built up. Not verbalizing this pain, sometimes even in an effort to protect the people around me, once again found its voice in more physical tension, nervous system dysregulation and random flareups. I needed to learn to acknowledge, embrace and accept all parts of myself, even the painful parts such as sadness and disappointment if I was going to get more healing.

Letting go and truly grieving was pivotal for stepping into my next phase of healing. It was painful and raw and vulnerable but I did myself (and my loved ones) a disservice with my lack of emotionally honesty around all the losses I had experienced and felt as part of my daily health journey. This honesty allowed me to finally express my anger with God at all those years that I had felt were lost. There were times when I couldn't pray (except for maybe a rant at God a time or two or three!) or read my Bible. Inviting loved ones into my grieving process enabled other people to hold me up in prayer as I worked through the pain.

It was an uncomfortable season but it also felt so good to finally be real! There was beauty and relief when I finally admitted where I was at and what I had gone through for over a decade and a half. Life didn't fall apart as I grieved. God didn't disappear and my loved ones were more supportive as I shared my pain. It was an incredible and painful time – and I overcame it! At a deeper level I knew that God would hold me up and could handle my pain, anger and sadness. He made me, He saw my tearful nights and heard my words over the years. And this honesty allowed me to begin healing in ways that I didn't know I needed.

Grieving may be need to become a part of your daily experience when you live with chronic illness or pain, particularly if you are dealing with limitations or disappointments related to how your illness affects how you can function every day. Setting aside some time every few days to express and engage with your emotions of anger, disappointment or sadness related to your physical health issues is something I would highly recommend in your healing journey. Yes, because it is honest, but more so, because this honesty allows you to then move on and experience other, more positive emotions throughout the day.

You don't need to be held captive to sadness and disappointment or anger. Emotions are meant to be experienced and released. Engage and release. The more you hold onto those negative emotions, the more you will get stuck in an on-going cycle of negativity feeding into whatever negative emotion you are feeling. This will slow your healing process.

Learning Self-Compassion

The second piece of emotional healing I want to address here is the important practice of self-compassion. Self-compassion can be extremely hard to practice particularly when your pattern has been to shut emotions down or tell yourself that you shouldn't feel a certain way. Just because an emotion may not 'make sense' or it feels embarrassing or uncomfortable does not make it wrong or worthy of your disregard. Growing in self-compassion builds emotional resiliency.

Self-compassion is extremely vulnerable – but this vulnerability is not weakness. It takes courage to face hard emotions, to face what is uncomfortable or unfamiliar. You may even feel unsafe initially as you engage with your emotions in this new way. You need to practice self-compassion so that you can develop a true curiosity around your emotions, exploring how you feel or what sensations they show up as in your body.

It is about creating a space where you are willing to be gentle with yourself in an uncomfortable place. This attitude is far more life-giving than a tendency to always judge why you feel this or that way, shutting emotions down, criticizing yourself or explaining negative or hard emotions away. Those behaviours will only feed into further physical, emotional and mental pain.

As I worked towards emotional health, I had to learn to stop speaking negative words or thinking negative thoughts around the emotions that came up. Journalling really helped me because it was a private space where I could express my 'irrational' emotions without any external judgment. It forced me to slow down and pay attention, even if it was just for 3 minutes when normally I wouldn't give any time to pay attention to myself.

Developing self-compassion isn't easy and it will take time and discipline. However, a lack of harshness and judgment towards yourself creates a greater sense of peace which impacts your body physically in ways beyond your ability to see in a given moment. It is truly life-giving, healing and affirming to yourself and to your body. It makes you feel safe at a deep level and in every sphere of your being which feeds into your physical sphere of health.

> *Self-compassion creates a greater sense of peace which impacts your body physically in ways beyond your ability to see in a given moment.*

This has benefits such as increased immune strength, more energy, better sleep and digestion and many other positive outcomes. The more you practice these skills, the more healing you bring to your physical body. God has created your body to heal but it really does require a holistic approach! You can learn to care for yourself, create space for yourself and love the person God created you to be with all your emotional highs and lows.

Reaping the Benefits from Emotional Healing

We all want a guarantee that the time and energy we devote to our emotional health will produce amazing health benefits, particularly if it involves delving into difficult areas! Although I cannot tell you specifically what the outcome will look like for you, I can tell you that there will be incredible benefits to investing in your emotional health as a regular discipline.

Recall how emotions can get stuck in the body, finding their voice in physical, mental or emotional symptoms. As you work through the emotional part of your healing you are attending to your body's voice that may have long been ignored. Paying attention to it's voice, creating space for it to be heard and being gentle with yourself provide an opportunity for your body to be heard and then cared for.

As you attend to your body's expression of disharmony and pain with its pattern of symptoms and create a new way of being, you are rewiring the brain into a calmer state of being, moving you into a parasympathetic state where you feel safe and less reactive. This creates a healing environment within the body. Although it may take time for those benefits to show up as your body learns a healthier way of being, you will generally find yourself less overwhelmed, less reactive, more emotionally stable and more resilient to future stress. This resiliency feeds into a body that is more adaptable when facing ongoing life stress and should noticeably reduce symptoms when flareups occur.

Working with a Christian counsellor helped me learn new skills around self-compassion, self-awareness and breaking emotional patterns that were impacting my health. At times, particularly in the beginning feeling and engaging with my emotions made me feel worse. I had to engage with a lot of 'negative' emotions and that was uncomfortable. I had to remind myself that *feeling uncomfortable did not mean it was bad*. I had to tell myself that with time I would see how healthier patterns in my emotional health would benefit me and the people around me.

As time has gone by, I have seen significant personal emotional growth and experienced the positive outcome of improved emotional health. I also see how my new emotional resilience has improved my body's reaction to stress, thereby reducing the physical symptoms of pain and inflammation.

The emotional investment has physical, emotional and mental rewards. This takes time and patience which is hard to come by when you want to heal. Remember that slowing down is essential. Stick it out and you will reap great rewards. If by the end of this workbook you still find that you have not gotten the health outcomes you are looking for, or you want more support right now to help break the physical patterns or expressions of your illness, it might be helpful to work with a health professional. Practitioners that address the energetic level and energetic patterning of dis-ease can be helpful for breaking and uprooting these physical patterns of expression.

As you become more emotionally healthy and resilient you can expect to see healing – decreased frequency and intensity of symptoms is a good sign!

Homeopathic medicine has an incredible ability to uproot patterns of physical expression of disease when the root cause is emotional or from past trauma even into childhood. Other medicines that also work within this arena include Chinese Acupuncture, Emotional Freedom Technique, Somatic

Experiencing, and EMDR (eye patterns and imaging to release trauma).

As you begin the Healing Questions for this section keep in mind that you start first from a place of compassion. You may find yourself getting triggered as you work through these questions and that's okay! Be patient with yourself and remind yourself that triggers are invitations to another area of healing. They are places of opportunity and potential and growth.

You may find yourself realizing that you need to work with a counsellor or therapist and need more than just these questions to heal or that you need to return again and again to the same questions as you uncover greater depth and clarity. It may start with looking back and simply acknowledging past trauma or your patterns of emotional behaviours. You will be surprised and delighted to encounter all of who God made you to be and find yourself overwhelmed by just how amazing your emotions truly are when you engage with them.

My goal with the following questions below is simple. Just start looking at, giving space to and voicing your emotions. It truly begins with paying attention to (sometimes to the uncomfortable) pieces of yourself that have previously been left or brushed aside. Then you start to learn to live with them, engage with them in a new way and ultimately thrive with them!

Speak truth over yourself and remind yourself what God says is true and this will have positive influence on your mind, body and spirit. The beauty of your healing journey is that it takes place on your schedule, when you are ready and able to deal with things. No one is rushing you. Remember to invite the Holy Spirit into this process as He is your Counsellor, your Truth-teller, your Comforter. Commit this emotional healing journey to Jesus as He knows your way and He is your Healer.

You've got this! (And even if you don't...God does!).

You will be surprised and delighted to encounter all of who God made you to be and find yourself overwhelmed by just how amazing your emotions truly are when you engage with them.

Healing Questions Part 2:

1. What thoughts or insights came up for you as you read though this chapter? Jot down anything that came up for you – past events, views, experiences with emotions that were uncomfortable/safe, etc.

2. How do you feel about your emotions, particularly the hard or negative ones?

   a. What words come to mind when you think about emotions and/or expressing your emotions? (Scary? Neutral? Safe?)

b. Are there emotions you tend to avoid, suppress or ignore or possibly fear? List them and describe how they make you feel. This might be a physical sensation or even bring up other emotions. Patiently and gently explore each emotion listed.

3. What or who has contributed to your views on or expression of emotions? Having insight into who or what has impacted your views on emotions can be helpful in healing. This is not about blaming but understanding how you formed some of your thinking around emotions and their expression.

4. Do you feel you can express your emotions freely and without judgment from yourself?

5. What holds you back from expressing or experiencing emotions? List all the things that are contributing to this.

6. List all the ways that you deal with or work through your emotions, both positive or negative? (shut down, repress, express them, blow up, talk to a friend, etc.)

7. Are there certain emotions that you feel uncomfortable expressing?

   a. What is it about those emotions that feels more comfortable or uncomfortable? Explore how you engage with the specific emotions that you feel uncomfortable.

8. Do you get angry, frustrated or irritable easily? What makes you truly angry?

9. Do other people's emotions trigger you? If yes, consider why that might be.

10. Do you notice that you develop health issues or symptoms or flareups when you are emotional or stressed out? If so, what emotion(s) seem to trigger these symptoms?

11. Are there specific situations/events or even a person that triggers your health symptoms? What symptoms do you experience? Pay attention to and write down the physical sensations you experience when you experience that trigger. (see Healing Exercises Part 2 #2 to learn more about how to do this)

12. Have you allowed yourself to grieve lost or disappointed hopes/dreams? If not, what's holding you back? (fear, shame, judgment – sit and explore why this might be, pray about it).

> Take some time to talk to God about the losses you've experienced. This is a time to fully express and feel. This probably won't be a one-time event. As the emotions come up allow yourself to feel them.
> One thing that I have found true of grief is that it does not look like you expect it would so be open to any expression of emotion or even no emotion or emotion showing up at random moments. Self-compassion is key here. Just being present to yourself and your feelings and not trying to rationalize them in the moment is good!

13. What are some ways you can grow in expressing your emotions? These don't have to be big steps. Some ideas: Acknowledging the emotion. Feeling the sensations in your body. Calling a trusted friend and sharing your feelings.

14. What are some ways you can grow in compassion with yourself? Think about the way you think about yourself, how you talk to or about yourself particularly when you are emotional or make a mistake. Words such as "I'm too.." indicate a lack of compassion. Jot down some ideas either from the reading or from your own thoughts.

Healing Exercises Part 2:

For this section I would like you to pick 2 or 3 of the following exercises and implement them in your life on a daily/regular basis. It's the regular practice of these that will have a beneficial impact on your health.

#1 - Journalling

Journalling is an amazing way to express yourself. Don't think you need to write paragraphs or that it has to make sense. The point is to create a space just for you where there is no judgment and where you can be 'heard.' When you are used to suppressing emotion or ignoring it it's essential to create a space (even if it's 3 minutes every evening) to give voice to yourself.

I found that the biggest reason I didn't want to journal was I didn't see the point of it or how it could possibly help me with my emotional health. As I journalled for a few minutes daily I found that the unloading of the few things I wrote down (thoughts, emotions, frustrations) created better emotional awareness for myself but also gave me more space in my life for other things and people. I wasn't as easily overwhelmed by other things because I had created space and time for me.

Some ideas that you can write about to get you started include: how you feel, things that are going on in your life, your hopes and dreams, Bible verses that speak to you, prayers from your heart, questions you have for God.

#2 - Paying attention

Take 5 minutes daily to sit or lie in a quiet, comfortable place. Close your eyes and just pay attention to your body. What do you feel? Give a voice to the emotion or feeling that is 'screaming' the loudest in that moment. This might look like: describing how it feels in the body, giving it a colour or a shape, what sensations does it give off, where is it located in the body. You can also see if there is any way to provide 'relief' to that sensation or visual – for example, if it appears like a big dome of black in your core that is putting so much pressure on you inside how can you relieve that pressure? Maybe it means blowing cold air into that space or letting it spew out of your mouth (this is all a mental picture).

#3 - Do something fun or creative!

Doodle, draw, paint, sew, read a good book, watch a comedic video. Do something that gets you laughing or relaxing. This is healing! If you don't have any hobbies now might be the time to try something new.

#4 – Learning to Identify your Emotion(s)

When you feel an emotion in the moment that you would normally shut down, pay attention to it in that moment rather than dismissing it.

1. **Identify the emotion(s).** This can take some time to learn as there can be multiple layers of emotion. If there are multiple emotions state them all out loud. Then choose to focus on ONE of them – maybe the one that is the most present or 'loud.' E.g. I am angry. I am sad. I am afraid.

2. **Respond to your emotion with compassion.** This is simply acknowledging the presence of that emotion without judgment. For example, you could say something like, "It's okay to be afraid. God sees me and is with me," or, "Of course I am afraid! I am dealing with something very new and outside of my comfort zone," or, "It makes sense I'm feeling discouraged. A lot of things haven't worked out lately."

3. **Care for your immediate needs.** This is about recognizing what your body needs in that given moment. Take a moment to ask yourself what you need in response to that emotion. Pay attention to what your body is feeling. For example, if you are feeling unsafe, you could ask yourself the question, "What do I need to feel safe?" As thoughts come to mind, put one or two of your ideas into practice. One idea that might make you feel safe may be hugging yourself or asking a loved one for a hug. It may be texting a friend and asking for prayer.

If you can't deal with the emotion right at that moment, you can do the following practice: acknowledge the emotion, (for example, you can say something like this, "I see that you are angry. I am not ignoring you but I cannot deal with you right this moment. I will return and care for you later." Then later you attend to that emotion. Allow yourself to feel it, express it in a safe place or to a safe person, use the steps in above.

#5 - Self-Compassion Skill Development:

If you tend to be quite hard on yourself or judgmental of your emotions then this might be a valuable practice. It's a simple awareness and acknowledgement of the presence of the emotion without judgment.

1. **Identify the emotion that you feel.**

2. **Get curious about the emotion you are feeling.** It's almost like stepping into the role of being an external observer. Visualize the emotion or give voice to how it feels in the body By creating this picture and/or describing the sensations you feel you are allowing yourself to experience the emotion. It isn't judgmental but shows genuine curiosity to all the sensations. Visualizing doesn't shut it down or ignore but gives the emotion a voice that might be a more comfortable way of expression or experiencing an emotion for you (e.g. a picture). Some questions that might help to move you into a place of curiosity about the emotion include:
   - What does this emotion feel like in my body?
   - What sensations do I feel with this emotion?
   - What colour or temperature or appearance could I give this emotion?

3. **Be intentional about the way you speak about the emotion or yourself when you are experiencing the emotion.**

4. **Speak encouraging words to yourself.** This might simply be affirming how you are feeling. "I feel sad and that's okay. It's been a hard day." Or "I feel angry because I was ignored. It's okay to be upset about this."

5. **Speak to a trusted person about what you are feeling.** An external view can give you a perspective that rarely judges. Think about how often you don't feel judgment when you see someone cry but when you cry you might feel judgment towards yourself! An outsider perspective might help realign expectations which can create more compassion with yourself.

Pause & Reflect

Let's pause for a moment. Part of your healing journey is celebrating the work you've done! It takes time and effort and intentionality to rest and to check in with how you feel. It takes effort to learn and practice a new skill. That is worthy of your attention.

....

Maybe you have learned something new about yourself. Maybe you've noticed a difference in how you feel or view yourself. It could be anything! The pausing and reflecting is an invitation for you to reflect on and celebrate the investment of your time and energy.

At this point, you may not feel any different at all and that's okay! Sometimes it takes months for the realities and truths of the work you do to take root and show their fruit. In my own experience with doing the spiritual and emotional work around my identity, I saw an immediate change in the way I viewed myself. I noticed that I was more confident in my value and the way I thought about myself. I knew that I deserved to be treated as a woman of value in my relationships. I stopped feeling like I was "too much." I could confidently say to myself that I was worth loving.

There were other pieces, specifically the emotional pieces, that took years for me to really see change in the way I wanted to see it, but I was proud of the work I did, knowing that it had positive influence on my overall health and wellbeing. Although I knew the emotional work needed to be done, I wasn't quite sure where I would end up at the end of it all. I kept telling myself it was going to be worth it and that I needed to keep going. I was proud of myself for delving into the hard places *when* I could handle it. (*When* is key here!)

I wasn't always ready to uncover or work through things and there were times when I needed months to even begin looking at different aspects of my past or present emotional pain. It is not uncommon that we lack the skills to integrate our emotional experiences into our adult life experiences when we didn't learn to work through our emotions as a child due to trauma or environments that didn't create space for us to do so. As a result, we can become overly rational or logical adults and continue to suppress our emotions. Inner child work is a helpful therapeutic approach that can help you learn to integrate your emotions into your daily life experience. This can be done with the help of a counsellor or therapist.

As time went on and I did inner child work with my counsellor, I was better able to show up and care for my emotional needs. It was an incredibly valuable experience – but it took time, patience, self-compassion and a lot of growth in self-awareness. The journalling and visualization exercises were very helpful to me!

Part of my healing journey was learning to cry, learning to cry in front of someone I trusted, learning to cry in front of strangers and just accepting it was what it was. I picked up a journal with the only intention of creating a moment in the day when it was just about me. It wasn't about what I wrote, insignificant or significant, but it was about creating space to just be with my self. Sometimes I wrote for long periods, sometimes short. I wrote about how I felt or I jotted down a prayer or a desire. I created space to see parts of myself – whatever was most pressing in that moment. Honestly, if anyone read that journal they might be struck by how inordinately boring, childish, selfish or ridiculous I was. But who cares?!

The point is that we all feel fear, anger, sadness, disappointment with ourselves, our loved ones and the world (and even God!) and it is completely okay to put it out there. A journal was a wonderful space for me because I wasn't hurting anyone or offending someone. I was being real, authentic and vulnerable and to be honest and I needed a space where I was present with me. It was a simple 5 minutes (or 2!) and sometimes it would be 20 minutes. I noticed as I sat with myself, jotting down this or that, I had more space for others, life and whatever was thrown my way that day including onset of new symptoms or a flare up. Creating that emotional space gave me the ability to have more grace with a flare up which would normally send me into overdrive 'fix-it' mode.

As you pause and reflect in this moment, feel free to give yourself a bit of time to consider about how you've invested in yourself and your healing to this date. Maybe you've started to journal. Maybe you actually cried for the first time in years or you didn't push aside the uncomfortable emotions you felt in a moment. Or maybe you did and you actually were aware that you did that. Set a new intention to pay attention and feel that emotion next time.

Journal any thoughts that come to mind about the things you've learned about yourself (the good, bad and ugly), the things that are still a work in progress, the goals you have for yourself mentally, emotionally, physically and spiritually, and maybe something you realize you need to invest in for the future! These might be a desire to see a therapist every few weeks or sign up for prayer ministry sessions or something else entirely, like learning to paint or crochet.

I am encouraging you to start something that will get you to stop for a moment and pay attention. Maybe you would like to lie down, close your eyes and listen to the thoughts going through your mind or the sensations in your body. Don't try to solve or fix them. Just acknowledge that they are there. See them. This is about creating space, paying attention and these are truly foundational skills to learn for healing to take place. You cannot heal unless you see what's going on.

Part 3

Don't let Trauma Hold You Hostage

*The Lord is close to the broken-hearted. -
Ps.34:18a*

Trauma is a hot topic today in the world of health and for good reason: it is an area that is being acknowledged for its power to influence your genetics and your overall health. Exploring and working through past and present trauma has become an *essential* piece of the healing equation as you pursue health and wellness. Having delved into your emotional health and built your skillset in this area in the previous section, I want to invite you into even deeper healing and a deeper level of self-awareness. Let's begin to get curious about how our physical health is impacted by our experience with trauma or life-altering experiences in the past.

Before you become afraid, paralyzed or even overwhelmed by this word 'trauma' or the thought of looking back at places of pain, I want to remind you that you have begun to build emotional resilience through your practice of the emotional exercises from part 1 and 2. You have more emotional health and resilience than you did previously and God is with you in this process.

I also want to be clear that I am not necessarily advocating that you take a deep dive into painful events (although you may need to do this with the help of a skilled therapist or counsellor), rather, I am encouraging you to get more curious about yourself. The emotional patterns or behaviours you have formed and use on a daily basis are often directly influenced by life-altering or traumatic events that occurred, even as far back as into childhood.

As you look back on these events, even broadly, you may see a pattern of physical symptoms coming through as a result of the emotional responses and patterns you established. You may begin to see how you started to suppress or ignore your emotions or emotional needs. You may remember that your body began experiencing physical symptoms after a difficult or life-altering event, such as developing a sore stomach, anxiety or headaches. You may even recall that those symptoms became more frequent as you went through puberty or another life-altering experience.

This section will help you become better attuned to your body's voice and your own needs as you look to heal. This does not mean that the work will be any less difficult or emotional; rather, your emotional skills will foster your capacity to work through trauma and your resiliency will help you work through the emotional impact more effectively.

The Nuances of Trauma

Listening to patients in my practice over the past few years and working towards my own healing, I have seen how extremely nuanced trauma can be. Understanding these nuances is important for uncovering and processing trauma, past and present.

Trauma can occur from physical, spiritual, emotional or mental experiences and events. Although, we commonly acknowledge the 'big' ones including abandonment, neglect, rape, sexual abuse, combat, physical abuse, or emotional abuse, it can also include things that we ourselves or others might think aren't or shouldn't be a big deal.

They are the 'small T' traumas that are often dismissed or forgotten. These 'small T' traumas might include accidents, acute illness (both your own or of a loved one), experiencing a natural disaster or an unwanted move, a moment of intense fear, chronic stress, bullying, living in an unsafe environment, an unexpected pregnancy, divorce, spiritual abuse, a shock or something else entirely. **The thread that runs through all trauma is that there is something tangible that we take away from this experience, that changes us and that unfortunately wounds us in some way that might not be visible or obvious until many years or decades later.**

Understanding and working through trauma is difficult for a variety of reasons beyond the obvious wounds that come from a life-altering experience. It is a much-needed skill that you learn how to approach *all* of your life experiences with curiosity, because as you work to heal from past trauma, you need to be open to the fact that trauma might show up in unexpected places in your past. This is because your *perception* of an event has influence over whether something is experienced as traumatic.

Your perception of an event is influenced by many personal and external factors. These play a part in how those events will shape you and your health both in the moment and long-term. Understanding this is a helpful concept and is important to your healing. This awareness creates space to look back on different life stages and life experiences with curiosity and openness, helping you to view past events with fresh eyes so that you do not miss out on areas that need healing. It can also create space for you to grow in compassion with yourself as your ability to work through past traumatic experiences may have been limited by things that were not necessarily within your power, ability or control in that season of your life.

Some examples of factors that influence your perception of an experience include your level of emotional health, your coping skills and cognitive abilities, your inherited hardwired stress response and your level of physical health at the time of an event. Other factors that also impact your perception of an event may include the amount of social support you have during that period of your life, your family environment, your spiritual life, your age and many other things. There are so many things factors that affect life on a day-to-day basis – some of which are within your control and many which are outside of your control.

Even what we might consider 'normal' life events can become traumatic experiences as the body's capacity or resiliency is undermined by spiritual, emotional, mental or physical factors. Some of these insidious or external factors that can undermine the body's resiliency or capacity can include: living with chronic pain, dealing with ongoing financial stress or living in an emotionally abusive situation. These factors seem insignificant but can become problematic to the body and there may be consequences that are often unrecognizably tied to that event. For example, if you are going through a seemingly 'normal' life event while undergoing a lot of stress, this normal life event can be processed by the body as trauma. This event then has the power to throw your whole system out of balance and disrupt your health.

One area that is often linked to negative health outcomes in adulthood is adverse childhood events, or childhood trauma. Children do not have a plethora of emotional and cognitive coping skills, thus making them more vulnerable during difficult life events. This can negatively influence their health both short-term and long-term. It is not uncommon that physical symptoms or mood disorders show themselves during or after adverse childhood experiences.

Childhood is filled with changes that are often beyond their control. Children experience many different adverse life events, such as parental divorce, financial instability, unavailability of food, long-term emotional or physical neglect, bullying, war, upheaval and more. When we consider how they lack cognitive and emotional skills to process and understand these events, it is unsurprising that these can impact them long-term. Adverse events in childhood can impact immunity and resiliency that can, later in life, form a weakened foundation for health and create increased potential for the development of disease.

As adults, we often fail to consider the burden of our childhood adverse events on our health which is then compounded by a lifetime of traumatic experiences that remain unhealed or ignored. Therefore, paying attention and giving space to explore how all these events, past and present, becomes a necessary part of your healing journey. These may have all played a part in contributing to your heal issues today. Some of these events may need to be processed and worked through to bring deep healing and greater physical and emotional resiliency moving forward.

The Physical Embodiment of Trauma

The need to process and work through trauma as you work towards healing is because trauma has the unfortunate ability to embed itself in our bodies at a physical level. This is often why physical, mental or emotional health issues appear after experiencing trauma. The body's immediate response to trauma is often visceral or instinctive, meaning our sympathetic nervous system (think fight or flight) takes over and the body responds in ways that are purely reactive so that we can survive or get through it.

After the event, those instinctive emotions such as shock, fear or anger that were experienced in that traumatic moment or event, can remain locked in the body tissues. This feeds into a pattern of ill health and might show up as chronic stiffness, tension, pain, digestive issues, headaches, anxiety and many other symptoms. Repeated and long-term stress on the body can switch the body into a chronic stress state causing nervous system dysregulation. This state is almost impossible to fully heal in.

The locking of trauma in the body tissues becomes particularly problematic on our mental, physical, spiritual and emotional health when we ignore or suppress the immediate emotional and after effects of trauma. When we suppress or ignore the effects of trauma on our bodies, we are more likely to struggle with an increase in inflammation and decreased immune health that can feed into poorer health outcomes.

When we shut our emotions down or don't deal with emotional impact of trauma, the body will find a way of expressing its pain through whatever means necessary. Simply, your symptoms, whether emotional, physical or mental, can be the body's way of voicing the dis-ease or disharmony felt from the unhealed trauma. Unexplained symptoms or the onset of a new disease when experiencing significant stress shows the body is overwhelmed and has reached its capacity.

Although the body has an amazing capacity to heal and respond to stress, traumas and undealt-with emotions, it can only do that for so long before health issues in various forms start rearing their ugly head. The development of unexplained symptoms or disease can even take place over days or several years as the body's ability to compensate or react to stress effectively gets weaker and weaker.

Ultimately, the body's expression of symptoms is reflective of its state of overwhelm and its internal struggle to bring the body and mind back into balance and harmony. This is not a 'good' or 'bad' thing but a normal response to overwhelm and chronic stress. Although, this may not be a problem for someone who is generally physically well, for those who grew up in chronically stressful environments, for those who are physically unwell or who have a pattern of emotional suppression or avoidance or lack healthy coping skills, these may increase risk of disease and lead to poor health outcomes.

Epigenetics is the fascinating study of how environmental factors affect genetic expression. Environmental factors, such as the way in which you were parented, emotional neglect, physical, mental and/or emotional abuse, growing up malnourished due to food insecurity and many other adverse childhood events, can actually alter your DNA and make you more susceptible to developing certain diseases and psychiatric conditions later in life.

Chronic inflammation can occur from experiencing significant life stressors, both in childhood and adulthood and can result in an increased risk of developing psychiatric and autoimmune diagnoses.[5] Research shows the link between experiencing adverse childhood events and the increased likelihood of developing an autoimmune disease in adulthood.

In fact, those who experienced 2 or more adverse events in childhood had a 70-100% increased risk of hospitalization from autoimmune-type disease.[6]

Trauma has profound health impact on a person but also on the health of their children and grandchildren. In fact, research shows how trauma experienced by your parents, whether it be a physical trauma like long-term malnutrition or psychological trauma such as war or forced immigration, can increase negative health outcomes in their grandchildren.[7] [8] [9] [10]Unfortunately, trauma has a far-reaching and powerful influence over your health.[11]

Healing from Trauma

It is a common response for people with health issues and unresolved trauma to create ease or peace in the body through suppression of symptoms or behaviours that distract them from the root issue. These can include medication use, addictive behaviours, drug or alcohol abuse, emotional suppression, eating disorders and more.

These efforts might bring temporary relief to symptoms but the suppression of symptoms will never bring about robust health, because the root issues are not being exposed, worked through and healed. Trauma then remains trapped in the body and the body will continue to find ways of expressing itself in dis-ease and emotional or mental disorders. Rather than viewing the body's symptoms as an enemy to overcome, view them as a friend who is telling you there is something wrong that needs your attention and care. Your job now is to do the work and uncover what is contributing to the expression of your symptoms so that healing can occur.

Be reassured that this does not mean you are a victim of circumstances and are powerless to heal from diseases or disorders or other symptoms. In fact, as we discussed in the section on emotions, your ability to work through emotions can have beneficial outcomes for your ability to work through and heal from trauma. You can break up the physical embedding of trauma in the body by working through the emotions or breaking emotional patterns developed as a result of trauma. This will bring deeper healing.

> *Rather than viewing the body's symptoms as an enemy to overcome, view them as a friend who is telling you there is something wrong that needs your attention and care.*

The work of building emotional capacity and resiliency can also help prevent new stressful life events from wreaking more havoc on your health. Your ability to rewire your brain and break nervous system dysregulation nourishes your body and enhances its ability to react to stressors. It can even alter its genetics, thereby you're reducing your chance of developing disease! That is a powerful encouragement to you as you work through the tough things!

As you begin to explore your life events and possible past traumas in this section, there will be questions that are intended to get you thinking about the onset of your symptoms or illness in relationship to those events and the related experience. Bringing awareness to all the factors that contribute to the experience and perception of trauma is a much-needed skill in healing. You need to understand that avoiding the difficult places and leaving them uncovered will affect your ability to heal.

I don't invite you into this section lightly. Ask God to guide you patiently and gently through this process, healing parts of your heart that need it and calming any fear. Ask people you trust to pray for you as you process through it. We all need help at times and that is an expected and normal part of life and healing. We don't have to or need to do this work alone. In fact, if there is significant trauma that you have left ignored in your past, I highly recommend that you get psychological support for your own healing.

For those of you who don't have anything in your past that you would consider trauma but you do have chronic disease, emotional or mental health issues or unexplained symptoms, this chapter is especially written with you in mind. There is almost certainly something or several somethings that have built up to create a foundation that is allowing your current health issues to reside in your body. As stated previously, even the experiences that your mother dealt with during pregnancy influences the foundations upon which your health is built.

Before you walk away feeling powerless to affect genetic changes that might be generations old or stem from childhood, I want to remind you that God is greater than your fears, your genetics or your abilities. He wants to bring healing to you and He does provide wonderful tools to get that healing. One thing that always encourages me to pursue healing is that the healing that you do will affect future generations – so you pursue healing even for them!

Peeling Back the Layers

I love the picture of health and wellness as a tree in soil. The tree is where your health is lived out. It is where the symptoms are expressed – it's the fruit that grows. The soil is the foundation upon which your health is built. When you fertilize, water and aerate the soil, the tree becomes healthier. Alternatively, the unhealthier the soil, the more likely you are to experience increasingly devastating or debilitating symptoms or diseases.

You can heal the soil and uproot tendencies that might contribute to your current symptoms or the possibility of developing future disease. You are not just the product of genetics. You can nourish your soil so that you become a healthier person! In homeopathy, we call the tendency to develop certain dis-eases, even from genetic influence, miasms. Tilling the soil and fertilizing it through investing in your emotional, mental, physical and spiritual health, you are investing in future wellness.

Healing is a layer-by-layer experience. You uncover and work through one trauma and then you might need to work on something else that pops up. The healing will get easier as you work through these layers. The emotional, spiritual and mental effects of working through one trauma has profound impact on your ability to resolve and heal from other traumas because you are building skills, resilience and health through the process. The healthier you are the quicker your body bounces back from past trauma and the stressors that you experience from day to day.

Trauma is complex and often requires a multi-faceted approach and on-going work to heal. It is not unusual for your symptoms to reappear or to flare up, making you feel worse mentally, physically and emotionally. In fact, this is NORMAL. It's like tearing off the bandage of an infected wound and excising the poison, so that the wound can finally begin the healing process.

This is why you have been encouraged to work through the way you view yourself and how you experience and process your emotions. These are building blocks that build spiritual, mental and emotional capacity so that when hard emotions flare up (and they will!), you can be gentle and compassionate with yourself. You have gained an understanding that emotions are not a negative experience that need to be suppressed or ignored, but are in fact, part of experiencing an abundant life.

Having a firm grasp on your identity as a valuable and deeply loved child of God is crucial as you work through trauma. This foundational truth serves as a daily or moment-by-moment reminder, helping you battle feelings or lies that tell you that you are defined by your past experiences or that you don't deserve better. You can heal.

If you haven't begun incorporating the healing exercises from the previous sections into your daily life, I'd highly recommend you do this before going any further. These exercises are tools to help support your body as you work through all the facets of trauma healing. They equip you with the skills to build resilience, they bring calm when overwhelmed, they will help you feel and process and express things in healthy ways. They can help move you from a sympathetic state of reactivity and stress to a place of calm.

Ultimately, they empower you to live from a place of harmony and peace. Although it may not initially feel like they are accomplishing much the science shows that they are powerful. Don't let the small unseen gains feed into the lie that they are ineffective or useless. Repeated practice of them will bring healing.

Journalling, deep breathing exercises, walks in nature, weight lifting, screaming, crying, verbalizing your trauma, developing and expressing compassion yourself, expressing your emotions as they come up, writing out the whole trauma experience multiple times (science has shown that as you do this repeatedly it becomes less emotionally intense), prayer ministry, talking to a trusted friend, visualizing your emotions or describing the sensations you feel in your body, inner child work, learning and doing a creative skill (knitting, painting, baking, drawing, etc.), listening to music are just a few of many therapeutic healing modalities. Try a few different types of these exercises or tools to see which ones work best for you.

There are also many books, videos and podcasts that can teach you different therapeutic techniques. I will also include a list of resources at the end of this chapter with a few different suggestions. Have some fun exploring and pick those which bring you life and joy.

External Support for Trauma Healing

Lastly, as you work through this section on trauma, I want to mention a few wonderful treatment modalities that can support your body and mind as you work toward healing. They are helpful in reducing and healing your symptoms on the physical, mental and emotional planes. Although I go into more detail about these modalities in the physical health section later in this book, energetic medicines such as homeopathic medicine, Chinese acupuncture and other bio-energetic modalities such as sound therapy, light therapy, Emotional Freedom Technique (EFT) and grounding can be especially useful.

They have the ability to break through energetic blockages in your body where trauma is stored, helping to disrupt these patterns of dis-ease and symptoms that your body has developed as a result of trauma. Some of these therapies, particularly homeopathic medicine, can also help remove the inherited tendency to developing diseases which may have stemmed from maternal trauma that was passed onto you.

Learning to pay attention to your behavioural and thought responses to stress is also very important in the pursuit of healing. If you tend to shut down emotionally, talk negatively to yourself about how you are feeling, suppress your emotions until a blow up occurs, don't talk about emotion because you are afraid of hurting people, you can't say no, or you have trouble setting healthy boundaries with others, you are in need of some healthier ways of addressing your emotions and past trauma. You may require professional outside support to help with accountability and learn new techniques or skills that go beyond what is covered in this book.

Most importantly, I'd really encourage you to pray and invite the Holy Spirit into this process – for guidance, for healing, for direction and for comfort. Ask the Holy Spirit to reveal any areas in your past or times of your life where you were negatively affected and ask if that area requires attention and care. God is the Great Physician and can restore you to wholeness. It may take time, therapy, pages and pages of journalling and hundreds of hours of quiet time but it is worth it to be healed fully. Every step you take, and every layer you uncover will provide deeper, more holistic healing which will in turn benefit your overall health.

The questions below can be triggering. This is okay! We often are uncomfortable with the idea that healing can involve pain but to truly heal we may need to experience some discomfort. This is not a sign of failure. This is a sign that you were made for more and you can still feel! Be patient with yourself. Get *CURIOUS*. Be compassionate with yourself. And remember you are not alone! God is with you and is committed to you more than you can every imagine!

Health Questions Part 3:

1. Jot down any thoughts that came to your mind as you read through this chapter.

2. Can you think of any monumental life changes and/or traumatic situations/events in your life? List them. Don't exclude things that seem 'small.' If they were emotionally triggering or life-altering to you they are significant.

> For thought: Life-altering events that might be a trauma for you: death of loved ones (or even people we've had a traumatic history with), unexpected pregnancy, retirement, moving, war, fears related to finances, separation from parents or mother during infancy due to sickness, bullying, relationships, divorce, job upheaval, spiritual abuse, insecurity or feeling unsafe particularly in childhood.

3. Looking back at question 2, are you aware of any impact these traumas had on you short-term and long-term? If yes, write down how they impacted you then and now (physical, mental, emotional, spiritual).

4. Do you feel you have fully worked through the emotional impact of each of the monumental life changes and/or traumatic situations/events you listed in question 2?

a. Have you allowed yourself to process and *feel* the emotions? Mentally processing through trauma is only one aspect of processing trauma. Allowing yourself to feel and experience the emotions that come up is also an essential part of healing. This is not always a one-time experience. For example, you may grieve over and over and this may relate to different parts of that trauma or something else entirely.

5. Write 5 words or phrases about yourself that you feel are tied into or came out of your difficult or traumatic life experiences. They could be words or phrases about your appearance, personality, skills, etc. Get curious and don't overthink this. What comes to mind organically?

a. Once you have your list expand on each of the 5 words or phrases. Write about what it means to you, how it has defined your sense of self. Be clear with the details.

b. These words or phrases have defined you because of your trauma. Take some time to consider: Imagine that the trauma did not define you. What else are you instead of those words? Write down what it would be like to be your whole, true self (consider the truths of your identity from Section 1).

6. Think back to when you started to develop your symptoms or illness. What was going on in your life? Were there any significant life changes or traumas that occurred in the months or weeks previously?

7. Looking back at #6, what kind of symptoms did you start experiencing initially? They could be physical, emotional or mental symptoms.

8. Did you ever deal with the emotional aspects of the trauma(s) related to your symptoms? If so, how or what did that look like? If not, now might be the time to begin this journey. Utilizing the Healing Exercises such as Journalling or working through #4 or #5 in the Healing Exercises Part 3 may be a good place to start. Consider professional support if needed as well.

9. Do you find that episodes of flareup of symptoms coincide with stresses in your life? If so, pay attention and write down if there are specific types of emotions or specific interactions or experiences or triggers that seemingly cause flare ups/symptoms.

10. How do you handle stressful experiences in your life?

11. As you have worked through these questions, how has your understanding of your health and trauma impacted how you experience or see the symptoms you experience? What emotions or thoughts does it bring up?

> Your stress response is a good indicator of whether your body is in a state of calm or over-reactivity. If you find yourself chronically overreactive, oversensitive or even physically irritated/inflamed to what are 'normal' life experiences, more practice of the healing exercises would benefit you.

12. Looking back on these questions, do you feel there are any events or emotions that might be worth revisiting/working through? You may need to consider emotional support from a Pastor, Counsellor or good friend as you work through some of these.

Further Thoughts

Traumatic experiences can be opportunities for Satan to plant lies in your mind. I am going to call these footholds or strongholds that have been created in relationship to these experiences. Footholds or strongholds that can result from trauma include thoughts of shame, fear, loss of worth, self-hatred, fears of abandonment, etc. or lies about your identity and value. I go into more detail about this in Part 6 as we look at spiritual health and its relation to physical health issues.

As you have worked through the questions in this section, there may be things that come up for you around the pain of past trauma and possibly around spiritual strongholds. Since you are on a journey to healing and wholeness take some time to be with Jesus to talk to Him about your pain and anything that has stemmed out of that trauma. The words that He speaks will ALWAYS speak life and hope. He never condemns – so if you hear words of condemnation, ask Him to clarify what you are hearing as sometimes we hear incorrectly or misunderstand.

You can spend time in silence or with worship music playing. Feel free to have your journal with you to write down things that come to mind as you sit with Him. He knows your pain and carries you in your hurts. He can heal every emotional and traumatic wound. He can free you from the footholds and strongholds of the enemy. Remember that you "have divine power to demolish strongholds" (2 Cor 4:10). Exercise your authority as a child of God.

A powerful way to be free of spiritual strongholds is through prayer. God will always meet you where you are at. He wants to bring peace, comfort and to restore hope to you. He desires to heal places where you have been wounded. Some ways you can pray through the pain of trauma and the breaking of strongholds include:

> Ask God for a picture in your mind about where He was when you were hurt (because He is always with you). He might give you a word, a song or a picture showing His Prescence with you in those moments. He never left you. Write down what you see, hear or feel.

> Pray through the trauma. Ask God to comfort and heal you, to reveal lies or strongholds that were planted in your life as a result of the trauma. Using the prayer below you can break agreement with those lies and ask Jesus to speak truth to those areas where lies or strongholds were created. Remember our God is in the business of wholeness – healing you physically, mentally, emotionally and spiritually. You may want to go through this prayer with a trusted Christian friend or ask friends to pray for you while you do this as spiritual protection and authority.

PRAYER:

Heavenly Father, You see and know my pain and painful experiences. You carried me then and you carry me now. I desire full healing in Jesus' Name. I ask that you expose the lies that I have believed about myself as a result of the trauma (spend time listening and see what you hear/see – you may already know what lies you have believed from this trauma). I repent of _____(the lie)_____ and break agreement with it in Jesus' name. I speak the truth of your word over myself that ____(truth – a Bible verse, a statement that is true of who you are in Christ)__. I declare that any spiritual footholds or strongholds of the enemy that were created as a result of this experience be broken now in the mighty name of Jesus. In Jesus' name and by the power of His blood I declare that I have been bought and paid for by the blood of Jesus. Thank you for your healing in Jesus' name. Amen.

Healing Exercises Part 3:

As you work through traumatic experiences you may find yourself reverting to ways of functioning or being that are indicative of a nervous system that is in the sympathetic state of fight, flight or freeze mode. Learning to calm yourself through the following exercises are a wonderful way of retraining your brain to heal the nervous system and rewiring it to the parasympathetic state. The parasympathetic state is more conducive to healing. With time and practice you can build emotional resilience and return your system to a harmonious state.

#1 - Movement:

Movement can be very calming and healing to the body. It can help redirect the focus you have on your emotions and center or ground you in the body. It was a way of paying attention to your emotional state through paying attention to the physical sensations that you experience. Walking, stretching, weight lifting, dancing or other forms of movement can be very therapeutic.

> ➤ Pay attention to the physical sensations that come up as you work through the emotion through movement. If you find yourself in your head this is not the purpose of this exercise. Get back into your body, experiencing the sensations of that emotion by asking yourself to describe what the emotion feels like, where it is in your body and what it looks like. You can give words to the emotions and its sensations by giving it colours, textures, shapes and more.

#2 - Hum or sing:

Humming and singing create vibration which in turn stimulates the vagus nerve. The vagus nerve can become overworked and lose its ability to communicate well particularly from long periods of illness, chronic stress or inflammation. Humming and singing (even gargling!) can help reset the vagus nerve and improve its tone which in turn helps your body return to a higher state of resiliency and calm.

> ➢ Humming should be such that there is a buzzing sensation felt.
> ➢ Try to hum or sing daily, in the shower or wherever you are for at least 3 minutes.
> ➢ Sing songs of victory over sin & Satan. Sing song of the power of Jesus over your circumstances.

#3 - Hug yourself gently.
You can also sway side to side while doing this promoting a sense of calm and safety.

#4 - Re-write the traumatic experience:

Taking time to write the traumatic experience can help release the emotional hold it has on you and bring different levels of healing. It is recommended to write out the experience a few different times. You could write it from the past tense and then in the present tense. Do this 2 or 3 times. With each writing you may find that you see different emotions, different details, have a different perspective. This can transform the way you experienced the event and bring a deeper level of healing.

#5 - Using a photo as a journal prompt: Choose a meaningful photo for yourself, ideally one with you in it. Use it as a prompt for your writing. You can include physical details (e.g. location, date) but you can also write about emotions that you were feeling or things that aren't seen. What led up to this moment? What was going on in life at that time? Allow this time to be a reflective time surrounding life events that had a profound impact on you. Explore your internal life and get curious. What comes up for you?

Pause & Reflect

You have just worked through one of the hardest parts of this book. I'm so proud of you! Be proud of yourself! Celebrate how much effort and time you've invested in a health journey. I hope that you are starting to come to understand how truly interconnected every part of you is and how essential pursuing wellness in every sphere is needed for healing!

It's possible you are already reaping some positive health benefits from the time you've invested and work you've done. Maybe you are just more aware of your symptoms and how they are linked to your past. Maybe you've integrated some new skills to calm your nervous system or work through tough emotions. Now you have some new perspective and hope that there can be more healing for you!

It's possible that you've come to realize that it's time to see that therapist or counsellor and get the support or skills you need to work through your emotions or trauma. I know that counselling can be costly but poor health is more costly in the long-term. If money is a concern, consider having one or two counselling sessions every few weeks for a 3-4 months. This can help give you a clear idea of what you need to work through on your own. You can also ask your counsellor for guidance or help in specific areas, such as building emotional awareness or setting boundaries, so that you are more prepared to do the work on your own. You can be an empowered advocate for yourself. You may need to ask your counsellor if she has any tips or direction for you based on what she sees from your conversations. Your journey is unique to you.

I would highly recommend journalling to everyone working through emotions, trauma and healing. It is a safe place to start learning how to recognize your emotions, express them without judgement and have a safe place to share and unload all the thoughts that you feel you can't share with others.

Most importantly, talk with your Heavenly Father about everything you are working through. He sees you where you are and His desire for you is freedom from your pain, your sickness and your bondage.

Reflect on the things you've worked through, how far you've come, some skills you learned or some new coping skills you've adopted. Write it down. Share it with a trusted friend. Celebration is a vital part of your healing. It's a time to celebrate!

Part 4

The Physical Sphere of Healing

My health may fail, and my spirit may grow weak, but God remains the strength of my heart; he is mine forever. – Ps. 73:26

This is probably the part of the book you have been waiting most eagerly for. Maybe you even decided to skip the first few chapters because you don't really care (or want!) to understand how identity, emotions and trauma play a part in a physical healing journey. If that is you, PLEASE, PLEASE go back! God created us beautifully, each part of our being intricately connected with each other.

Your physical health plays an instrumental role in your mental and emotional health and vice versa. The role they play and the interaction between the spheres is powerful yet often unexplored or untended. One area of unwellness *will* have impact on another area – even sometimes 'borrowing' energy from another area that is healthier so that the unwell or injured part can keep functioning to some degree.

If you want to truly heal, doing the emotional work is essential. I cannot say that enough. DOING THE EMOTIONAL WORK IS ESSENTIAL to your healing. You may not see its value yet, but you have laid the groundwork for a calmer over-all state of being, a nervous system no longer in fight or flight or freeze, a more robust immune system and many more benefits.

You are creating the space for yourself to be in a state of harmony rather than dis-ease and you have developed skills to increase your body's resiliency and adaptability. You want to move from dis-ease or disequilibrium to ease and harmony in every sphere so that the balance will create health and healing.

The positive outcome of choosing to function from a state of rest and incorporating a mindset shift around your value and worth, learning new skills to support a healthy nervous system and working through emotions and past trauma will benefit your body's ability to digest food properly, absorb nutrients and vitamins, sleep more soundly, boost your immunity and mood and generally heal.

Physical health is only one aspect of your health and wellness and it is frequently the area that gets the most attention when dealing with chronic disease or health issues or unexplained symptoms. That's no surprise of course! This is in part due to the fact that it seems to be the easiest thing to modify on our own. In addition, since it's the physical issues that are causing the problems and can really be the most 'bothersome' when it is out of balance, it seems to make sense to fix the thing that is so obviously broken.

Our healthcare system and society have conditioned us to think that the physical work or lifestyle modifications are the main way to achieving health. Typically, when our lifestyle modifications of diet or exercise no longer get us the health we want or fail to reduce the symptoms, we try a new diet, supplement, or therapy because we have been trained that this is the way to health.

This approach neglects the deeper work of healing our emotional trauma, the unhealthy emotional patterns and behaviours and the underlying sympathetic state that are bodies have become adept at functioning in. We want quick results and the physical work often brings the quickest results often avoiding the deeper, root-cause, holistic approach that addresses the physical, mental, emotional and spiritual.

I believe that we often only pursue physical healing for physical issues is because it can be much easier to continue in a state of emotional or spiritual dysfunction than function with physical dysfunction or ongoing symptoms. There is also something about physical pain and discomfort that makes doing the emotional work seem useless or irrelevant.

Changing the way we think, how we approach our life and dreams and deal with stress is countercultural and is much harder than cutting sugar, incorporating a new exercise regimen or taking new supplements. **We want to do rather than learn a new way of being.** There is just something about *doing* that seems easier and more 'productive' than changing the way we think, and to be honest, in my own healing journey I would say that this has often been true of how I thought about health.

The physical changes are much easier to do and, in my way of thinking, have the most direct link to my symptoms with the most immediate impact on my flareups. I also lacked the skills to do the emotional work and there were more resources out there that equipped me to keep changing the physical aspects of my lifestyle. The work of changing the physical sphere seems much easier to attain and is often more visible than doing the invisible work of healing our way of thinking about ourselves, uncovering trauma, learning a new way of dealing with our emotions or incorporating rest into a life where productivity and business is ingrained as the best way to function.

There are times when health issues are purely a physical problem such as when there is a deficiency of some mineral or vitamin, mold toxicity, parasites or worms or reduced health from a lifetime of bad eating habits. There may have been physical trauma from an accident, a vaccine injury, damage from parasites in the body or just an accumulation of poor lifestyle choices. These are physical problems than can be addressed through dietary or lifestyle changes.

However, robust physical health and the ability to heal rapidly and effectively from physical injury is more effective when you have taken care of the health of every part of you. Investing in every sphere of your health is akin to pouring nutrients into the soil on which physical health is based. In fact, **susceptibility to certain diseases, cancers, parasites and more are impacted by the health of the emotional and mental spheres!** This concept can be difficult to understand but it is fundamental when you truly want to heal.

Susceptibility to certain diseases, cancers, parasites and more are impacted by the health of the emotional and mental spheres.

You have probably experienced how you are more likely to get sick when you are stressed or after a stressful event which speaks to the role your emotional health and resiliency plays in your physical health. This is also true in situations where physical injury has happened and although tests show no physical damage or physical trauma remaining, patients continue to experience chronic pain. Our emotions are connected through our nervous system to the physical experience of that trauma and we need emotional healing related to that trauma to fully heal the physical pain. There is an inseparable link between the emotional impact of trauma and your physical symptoms. Pain patterns and physical symptoms can be 'uprooted' and healed through the combined approach of physical treatment and release of the emotional impact of that trauma.

The questions in this section include those that are part of the intake process in my consulting business. I'd encourage you to pause and reflect here, to stop and pay attention to yourself. This needs to be a part of regular life whether you are feeling well or unwell. Healing begins when you stop and pay attention. Start paying attention to your body and to your symptoms in a way you've probably never done before. Your body has its own unique language and you need to become familiar with it.

The questions in this chapter should be done over days or weeks and when your symptoms change again. Learn to pay attention to your body's voice. You cannot heal what you do not know. Maybe you are hyperaware of every tingle, spark and pain in your body but in my experience, most people aren't aware and lack the language to describe their experience because they haven't mattered to those treating them.

The questions around settings goals are there to stimulate some thinking around what you hope to gain or work towards in your healing journey. We often neglect goalsetting when it comes to health because no one has asked us what they are or to break them down. It's time to make this a part of your healing journey! Make them measurable and achievable so you can celebrate when you get there. Understanding how your goals relate to all of you is part of this exercise as well so that you begin seeing how interconnected everything is. Goal setting also lets you see how you have healed and celebrate your wins.

As you complete this section check-in with yourself about how realistic your health goals are given your level of health, the amount of water you drink, the exercise you do (or don't do), the food you ingest (quantity, quality, type), the time you give to your self-care and healing exercises, the journalling and other forms of emotional work. Don't be afraid to challenge yourself too. Look at the obstacles that stand in your way to achieving health and consider what life changes or supports might need to be put into place to begin a discipline of healthy habits.

Lastly, even though you don't' have a coach in front of you to respond to your answers, see this as an invitation to explore areas where you can grow with regards to each question.

Healing Questions Part 4:

What do you want to specifically achieve in this healing process? These goals can be physical, emotional, mental or spiritual. (Be as specific as possible – for example, I want to be able to go for a walk around the block, I want to half my pain medication use, I want to get pregnant, I want to make it through the morning without a panic attack, I want to speak 5 positive words over myself a day.)

1.
2.
3.

When you've achieved the goals you just listed above, what would that look like for you (be specific):

Emotionally:

Financially:

Physically:

Relationally:

Spiritually:

What are you most frustrated about with regards to your health?

What are you happiest about with regards to your health?

What do you **most want to change** for yourself in healing/to be healthy?

What do you feel are some obstacles to you achieving the level of health you want? (energy, focus, accountability, emotions, family pressure, etc.)

What do you wish you could do now that you are not able to do due to your level of health? (run for 20 min., go on a trip and be able to walk around, play with your kids)

On a scale of 1-10 (10 being lots), how much stress is in your life right now?

What currently causes you stress (what are your triggers)?

What typically motivates you to achieve your goals (rewards, determination, children, aligning with your values, etc.)?

What do you do for self-care? Include the exercises you have learned in this workbook as well.

On a scale of 1-10 (10 being most effort) how are you in performing self-care?

Do you perform any physical activity/exercise? If so, what type and how often?

How would you describe your sleep quality on a scale of 1-10? (1 is very poor, 10 is excellent). Describe any issues if any are present.

What medications & supplements, if any, are you currently taking and why?

Please list ANY medical condition (diagnosed or undiagnosed) and symptoms you have both past AND present. Take some time to go through all your health issues starting in childhood into adulthood.

Be specific as specific as possible and describe every single symptom you CURRENTLY experience with as much detail as possible. Describe the pain (aching, biting, burning, cramping, etc.), the time of day/night, what makes it feel better or worse (heat, cold, certain weather, foods, eating, drinking, etc.). Consider using Appendix D on page 241 or using a calendar to detect patterns.

What have you noticed makes your symptoms feel better or worse? (sleep, heat, sunlight, certain foods, exercises, etc.)

What are you currently doing to heal/stay as healthy as possible?

You may want to keep a nutrition and exercise log for a week to get a perspective of your nutrition and activity levels (see Appendix B & C on pages 237 & 239 for these items). Don't change your habits while you do this. <u>Let this be an accurate reflection of how you live and eat.</u> Based on a week's log consider the following questions:

How much water do I drink daily? Do I drink enough water?

Do I eat enough protein? Healthy fats? Fruits? Vegetables? Healthy carbohydrates?

Do I eat a lot of processed or sugary foods? Are there areas I could reduce my intake or specific foods I could cut out?

Can I add in new foods that would: increase protein? my fiber? Fruit & vegetable intake?

Do I eat enough calories for my body weight & activity level? (I find a lot of women undereat as our culture puts a lot of pressure on women to be small/thin).

Can I increase my activity level? Incorporate stretching?

What motivates me to eat healthy? To be active?

Pause & Reflect

You have done some amazing work! Your body needs a voice and you just made space and time to vocalize your body's aches, pains and symptoms and your heart's desires and goals around your health. This is HARD work but essential. Slowing down, sitting with that pain (physical mental or emotional) and you expressing what you may have never vocalized to yourself or anyone with all the details is a truly important step in the healing process! **Remember you cannot heal what you do not know.**

Another reason I had you write down all your symptoms in detail and set goals is because as we heal, we forget (naturally!) where we were and don't realize the healing we did. That's because health is something we don't think about when we are well and forgetting the pain of the past is part of that healing. However, for you to heal you need to be able to see where you were and where you are going.

Now, take a moment and celebrate yourself. Look at what you have done, the time and money you have invested in your health and healing! One step or 30 steps are better than none. Healing is truly one step at a time.

Write down something you learned about yourself from the questions you just did. This might be an awareness of how much pain you function with on a daily basis or a celebration that you are still capable of dreaming for more or how far your body has taken you in spite of the pain or dysfunction. There are no wrong answers.

Part 5:

The 10 Tenets of Health & Healing

*Heal me, LORD, and I will be healed; save me
and I will be saved, for you are the one I praise.
– Jer. 17:14*

You may be wondering why I had you write everything down in so much detail in the previous exercises. The body speaks through your symptoms. How can you heal what you don't even acknowledge or know about yourself? Diseases, unexplained symptoms and many mental/emotional disorders have some relation to your emotional health, past trauma, undealt with emotions and poor lifestyle choices.

Although the body has an amazing healing ability and capacity to deal with stress, trauma and suppressed emotion, it can only do that for so long before physical symptoms (in the form of anxiety, pain, digestive issues, etc.) start rearing their ugly head. Sometimes this process can take years and sometimes this can take days.

Our typical approach to healing is to focus on modifying our physical health. There are several reasons for this. One, because it can sometimes be the 'easiest' thing to work with. Two, it is often where we see the quickest results and that is rewarding in and of itself. Three, it is an area where *you* can build the skills and have some element of control: *you* are capable of changing your diet, selecting a great supplement or incorporating an exercise regimen. Fourth, the emotional work can seem unrelated to your physical symptoms. And fifth, it can be much easier and more affordable to get help for physical issues than the emotional.

We live in a system where our physical health often takes precedence over emotional health and there is often very little incentive or understanding of how to personally start addressing the connection between the two as you work toward healing. There is also stigma around seeing a counsellor, maybe less so today than 30 years ago, and if you see a psychiatrist…well that's often prescribed only when someone is considered really mentally or emotionally unwell.

Despite our access to incredible amounts of information around health and wellness, it is mindboggling to me how poorly equipped we are to deal with our physical health issues let alone our emotional health. We really need to learn to heal a basic understanding of our bodies and the connection between every sphere. We need to develop basic skills to support health in every sphere so that stress and trauma don't send our bodies into a tail spin of inflammation, emotional distress, chronic pain and unexplained symptoms.

You started this section discussing facts related to your physical health – your symptoms, your goals, your lifestyle choices. You need to understand how you function, patterns of behaviour so that you can continue to develop lifestyle habits that will contribute to wellness. These are the simple ones such as exercise, nutritional choices, stress techniques and sleep. I will go into someone detail on each of the aforementioned below as well as some further foundational lifestyle choices that will impart health.

Many of these recommendations are generally helpful for most people but obviously a discussion with a doctor or qualified health practitioner if you are dealing with certain health conditions might be required. These are tips and suggestions and do not replace medical advice. The point is not to harm or overwhelm you but to help. I would also like to recognize that not everyone is in the financial place to even do these things. Maybe you don't even have the energy to choose to make changes in every area. Pick one or two then! Any step is a step to healing and they do make a difference.

We live in an extremely toxin rich world – the air we breathe, the food we eat, the things we put on our skin – and avoiding the world is not possible. We need to pick and choose on a daily basis what we can handle, what we can afford and how much energy we can invest in these lifestyle choices. So, if you choose to focus on water that's totally ok! The natural health world is overwhelming and more advice is readily available if you want to find it. However, remember that you DO NOT WALK IN FEAR!

You do your best to nourish yours and your family's bodies and you function within your limitations and that is totally okay! Don't let fear control your choices because fear impacts our health. **God is bigger than the choices you make and loves that you are choosing health today in the simple ways you do it!**

And as a reminder, we all have areas we just choose to live and 'let go' – I get my hair coloured 1-2x/year and I KNOW that it is toxic and I at this point still choose to do this. This is one area where I find beauty and fun. Others might love painting their nails or having the occasional Starbucks latte with the sugar and artificial flavours. We need to LIVE because joy comes from living and enjoying life and that is essential to health.

This section could be a whole book in and of itself. In fact, you probably can find a book written on each section alone. The point of this section is to give a basic, yet foundational starting point that will have positive impact that costs you the price of this workbook and what you choose to invest. 😊 I will share some of my favourite products or brands but don't feel limited to my suggestions!

There are a lot of specialists, doctors, natural medicine professionals, therapists, therapies, treatments and more out there. There is a lot of free information and suggestions and protocols on how to heal this or that. The things I suggest as basic tenets to physical health are based on my 15+ years working in healthcare and my personal experience with different modalities and therapists as I navigated my own health issues. There is enough research out there and books written on each of the topics found so if you want more information on specific things please go find and read them.

This workbook is about creating ease in your search for health, making it easy to read, easy to access and hopefully easy to implement so my recommendations are as brief as I could possibly make them. Don't underestimate the power of some of these suggestions because they seem too simple. We have lost so much connection to nature and to ourselves in this overcomplicated world that have actual, powerful healing influence.

Tenet #1: Water & Hydration

Our bodies are mostly made of water and so it's little surprise that water has a noteworthy part in health and healing. Too many of us underestimate the healing power of water and the function it plays a part in within your body. Water energizes, plumps, hydrates, mineralizes and structures every single cell, and ultimately plays a starring role in the communication and function of between every cell, to name just a few things. The water in the body is, at a cellular level, structured into a liquid crystal formation, similar to how the screen of your cell phone works, which supports the communication of all kinds of information throughout your body. Water is vital to life.

The water we drink straight from our taps often contains little to no minerals, the remnants of many medications (think flushed birth control pills, antibiotics, painkillers, etc.), chemicals such as fluoride and chlorine, heavy metals and many other toxins.

Due to the overwhelming amount of toxins in our water, good filtration, particularly of drinking water is a good idea. Filtered, mineralized water is even an even better choice and is not merely a recommendation but an essential piece of your health.

I would highly recommend that you do not ingest city tap water without any type of filtration. Every city or township has different contaminants that are added to their water; as such every household will have different needs for what type of filtration would be beneficial. Well water also needs to be tested and properly filtered as there can be different bacteria in the water.

Water filtration in your home can be for your drinking water alone or you can install a whole system filter. A whole system product filters all water coming into your home so even your bath and shower water are filtered. If that is too costly it is possible to purchase filters that fit on shower heads and faucets for bathing as chemicals in your water are absorbed through the skin. Do what you need with regards to your health and that which is within your budget.

> **To keep in mind:** Every filtration system has different benefits or shortcomings. For example, Reverse Osmosis, a popular water filtration system, removes all minerals and so they must be added in before using it for drinking. This system also has significant water waste. Make sure you do your research when selecting a water filtration system!

FILTRATION

Generally, a quality water filter is worth every penny and shouldn't be too expensive an investment long-term, particularly when compared to buying bottled water. Filters are usually changed yearly within a reasonable budget. I'd recommend looking for a brand that you can afford, has easily accessible parts and filters for purchase within your country, reliable customer service and lots of positive reviews.

Lastly, do not be afraid to ask for scientific literature to support their claims around their water filtration and water quality. You will find many people recommending various filters, but filtration needs will depend on where you live and whether you are on city or well water. I personally do not have specific suggestions for brands.

MINERALIZATION

The addition of minerals to your water is an easy way to support health and cellular function. Too many of us are mineral deficient which reduces the cell's ability to function efficiently which can contribute to muscle cramps and aches, sluggishness, fatigue and more. Pay particular attention to adding minerals when you sweat, are in hot climates or exercise.

Drinking unmineralized water actually leaches your body of minerals and worsens mineral deficiency. If you find that you drink a lot of water and never feel hydrated or you drink water with minerals and still feel dehydrated you are most likely mineral deficient and need to supplement silica as this specific mineral is essential for helping with the absorption of minerals.

Minerals can be added to your water filtration system with a mineralizer specific to your filtration system or you can easily add 1/8 - ¼ tsp of Redmond's Sea Salt or other high mineral salt to a cup of water. If you are adding salt separately **do not use iodized salt as it is NOT mineral rich**. There are many mineral-rich supplements packets that can be added separately to water for convenience but they are rarely necessary and quite expensive.

ADEQUATE WATER INTAKE

Lastly, and most importantly, ensure you are drinking enough water. Water without minerals will actually deplete your body's minerals store and you may find yourself thirsty in spite of drinking 'enough.' Personal water needs vary and depend on how much coffee, alcohol and other dehydrating beverages you consume, as well as your activity levels and how much you sweat.

When consuming dehydrating beverages, exercising or sweating more, you need to go above and beyond the recommended 6-8 8oz. glasses of water a day. Signs of dehydration can include: constipation, dry skin, dry eyes, dry mouth, dark circles under the eyes, brain fog, low energy, muscle cramping, dark urine, headaches, dizziness, confusion. Remember that dehydration can occur even with adequate water intake – if that is the case – ensure you increase your intake of minerals.

Tenet #2: Reduce your Toxic Load

Toxins fill our world. Unfortunately, you can't escape them entirely so learn to recognize the toxins in your life and in your lifestyle choices and make an effort to reduce them where you can. Toxins can be sourced from (but not limited to): noise pollution, air pollution, skin products, cleaning products, water, food, the containers we use to cook, store and reheat food, electromagnetic (EMF) pollution (Wi-Fi, cell phones, 5G towers) and light pollution.

Every toxin you are exposed to has to be eliminated by the body. This places a heavy burden on your liver and other organs which is why I recommend everyone supports organ function and drainage. I have written more on this in Tenet #7.

For now, let's focus on reducing and eliminating the toxins we are exposed to, ingest or utilize in our daily lives. What I have written is not an exhaustive list of ideas but will hopefully give you a place to start or stimulate some thoughts around how you might start reducing toxins in your environment and daily life.

LIGHT POLLUTION

Light pollution is excessive or unwanted artificial light. Artificial light affects our health by disrupting our circadian rhythm, sleep cycles and hormone production which in turn affects our mood, increases systemic inflammation and impacts the body in a myriad of unwanted ways.

I'd recommend that you consider wearing blue light glasses particularly at night or if using the computer for long periods of time in the day. Dim the lights at night to promote sleep, avoid screens 1-2 hours before bedtime, adjust your phone and computer screen to night mode to reduce blue light in the evening, avoid fluorescent light bulbs and LED light bulbs in your home if you can and consider using full spectrum light bulbs in the house.

Exposure to early morning sunlight and sunset helps to support your body's natural rhythms and is an easy thing to integrate into daily life. Even if it's not full sunlight or overcast, it is always a good idea to get outdoors for natural light exposure. You may need to purchase a light therapy box to support your circadian rhythm during winter months if you find your mood or sleep is seriously impacted.

See Appendix A for info on purchasing full spectrum light bulbs.

AIR POLLUTION

Air pollution is an often-forgotten source of toxins to the body. It can seem like a problem outside of our control, particularly if you live in the city but there are ways of protecting yourself and reducing air pollution in your environment. Those with respiratory issues, allergies, frequent exposure to wildfires or other airborne toxins such as those working in nail salons, hair salons and those who own pets should consider increasing support.

Anything you breathe in needs to be purified by the body and the liver again plays a particular role in breaking down inhaled toxins. That is also why I would recommend additional support and regular drainage of the liver if the previously mentioned describes your situation. See Tenet #7 to learn more about organ drainage.

- Purify your air especially if dust and seasonal allergies are a problem for you or you have respiratory issues concerns.
- Pet hair and dander can contribute to air pollution so air filtration is recommended, along with frequent vacuuming.
- Deal with mold issues in your home and shower professionally or ensure that you are using a proper mask and cleaning products as spores can be released and inhaled causing systemic health issues. Do not use bleach on mold! This only changes its colour but does not actually address the mold itself.
- Regularly dust and vacuum.
- Wash your sheets every 1-2 weeks, blankets and pillows every 3-6 months and even more frequently if you share a bed with pets or have respiratory issues. Replace pillows every 1-2 years.
- Avoid using air purifiers or artificial scents. Use soy or beeswax candles as other candles have negative health effects and artificial scents can irritate the respiratory system.
- Remember to change your furnace air filter – every 20-45 days particularly with respiratory issues or when living with pets!

FOOD CONTAMINATION

Food is a major source of contamination and toxin exposure. Being vigilant to what you ingest, how you prepare and store food and how you cook your food can have small but beneficial health outcomes.

- Aim to cook more meals at home or try your hand out at baking to reduce intake of processed foods which contain a lot of chemicals to keep things 'fresh'.

- Avoid using seed oils as much as possible (canola, grapeseed, sunflower, corn, cottonseed, peanut, etc.) and instead choose butter, ghee, tallow, coconut oil or olive oil. Oils do go rancid so use before expiration.
- Nuts & seeds should be stored in the fridge or freezer to prolong shelf-life.
- When baking at home, put half the recommended amount of processed sugar that the recipe calls for or replace with a natural alternative such as coconut sugar, honey or maple syrup.
- Try purchasing organic fruits and veggies or, if cost is an issue, purchase veggies and fruits that are lower in pesticides. The Environmental Working Group website (Appendix A) has a list of which fruits/veggies are higher in pesticides that year and are a great source of information for which food and body products contain more chemicals.
- Avoid heating food in plastic containers which leach microplastics into the food we ingest.
- Avoid Teflon-coated cookware and switch to cast iron or ceramic cookware. This goes for appliances such as slow cookers and air fryers as well. This will reduce exposure to chemicals such as BPA, PFOA, and PFA.
- Invest in reusable water bottles that are metal or glass.
- Drinking from disposable cups handed out by local coffee shop also increases toxic load due to the lining of the cups leaching into beverages. Try to keep a reusable cup on hand.

ELECTROMAGNETIC POLLUTION

Although electromagnetic pollution doesn't get talked about as much as it should, this is an opportunity to consider the impact of electromagnetic frequencies (EMF) on health. I will discuss this further in Tenet #9 but I will share a few ways to reduce unhealthy EMF exposure here.

- Turn the WIFI off at night (put it on an automatic timer switch so you don't forget).
- Sleep with cell phones on airplane mode or off entirely.
- Don't work with the laptop directly on your lap or body.
- Earbuds with Bluetooth contribute to EMF pollution as can holding your cell phone directly to your ear. Consider using earbuds with a wire or taking a call with the speaker on.
- Avoid putting the cellphone directly on your body particularly when walking around with it. Avoid holding your cell phone in general.
- You can purchase EMF shields that prevent EMF radiation and thereby protect your body.
- Grounding mats can be purchased to place laptops or computers on. I put my keyboard on a grounding mat.
- Grounding sheets which help protect your body from the disruption of EMF. Grounding devices are especially beneficial for those sensitive to EMF. Although I believe more people are sensitive to EMFs than we are aware of, this is probably in part due to the lack of research available about the health effects of EMF on the human body.

SKIN, HAIR & BODY TOXINS

We know that what we put on our bodies - the clothes we wear, the skin and hair products, the deodorants and the fabric cleaners – are absorbed by our bodies. A simple rule around skin, hair and body products are: **if you wouldn't eat it, don't put it on your skin**.

Here are a few ways to reduce skin and body toxins.
- Stop getting your nails done weekly. Ceramics, Gels and regular nail polish all leach chemicals into the body that have negative effects on hormones, can be carcinogenic

and allergenic, to name just a few problems with nail polish.
- Consider not dying your hair as often to cover the greys or switch to a natural henna dye.
- Fluoride in toothpaste is a hot topic. I tend to avoid fluoridated toothpaste entirely and choose natural brands. Daily brushing, flossing and a high-quality diet has the biggest impact on your oral health. Oil pulling with 1 tbsp of organic coconut or sesame oil 2-4x/week can be helpful to improve gum health and improve your oral microbiome.
- Anti-perspirants should be avoided at all costs. Switch to a deodorant instead, or even better, choose a natural brand. Some natural brands contain baking soda which can aggravate certain peoples skin.
- Use natural detergents and dryer balls instead of dryer sheets (these are especially toxic).
- Invest in linen or cotton pjs or sheets so that you sleep in fibres that are better for your body. Man-made fibres such as polyester reduce your body's natural frequency and can increase inflammation.
- Try making your own natural cleaning products. Baking soda, vinegar, essential oils, Dr. Bronner's Castille soap and many other options are available out there. It is not difficult or expensive to find natural cleaning products in most stores. See Appendix A to source different natural cleaning products.
- As a general rule – the more odorous the product (even pleasant odours!) the bigger the toxic burden on your body. This pertains to bathroom sprays, soaps, car scents/deodorizers, plugs that release scents, etc. Natural essential oils are okay.

- Natural skin care is quite affordable and there a lot of options out there. Natural health stores often carry full ranges of skincare, makeup products, soaps and more. The natural skincare market is constantly growing so you'll have a multitude of choices for your different skincare needs. You may need to try different brands and products as people react differently to items.
- Menstrual products: An area of a lot of hidden toxins, consider buying reusable organic pads or underwear. If using tampons or disposable pads, aim for organic cotton. Try out the Diva cup or other menstrual device.

Natural Skin Care Suggestions:

Products such as beef tallow, jojoba oil, castor oil, coconut oil, shea butter, cocoa butter and more can be wonderful body and face moisturizers depending on your needs.

If you struggle with blocked pores from oils you can look up the comedogenic rating on google to find which ones might work best for you. Skin care is highly individual so it can take some time and trying out a few different products to find what works for you.

Perfumes can be replaced by essential oil blends which have a double benefit of promoting mood, hormone health, relaxation and more depending on what you choose.

> Switch to more natural brand of shampoo and conditioner. Shampoo/Conditioning products from Live Clean are a great option but there are many other options such as shampoo and conditioner bars.
>
> If you like dry shampoo you can either make your own or try a brand such Acure or Luna Nectar that avoid butane and propane. Avoid using chemical SPF if possible. Use mineral based sunscreens as needed and/or hats.
>
> See Appendix A for Apps that will give you info on toxicity ratings by scanning the barcode. Very convenient while shopping!

Tenet #3: Sleep

It won't come as a surprise that sleep is foundational to health and healing. It is a time when we heal and rejuvenate mentally, emotionally and physically. Having suffered from severe insomnia I know how poor sleep impacts every facet of life. So, let's talk about things that impact our sleep and what it might look like to improve your sleep. Maybe you will have already tried all of the suggestions or a few and they haven't worked. It might be time to try a new combo of suggestions or to see a sleep professional.

Finding someone to work with you who will listen to your concerns and be open-minded to the possibility that something unexpected could be contributing to poor sleep can be difficult. A functional medicine doctor, homeopath or naturopathic doctor might also be the person with a more openminded approach when it comes to recognizing and treating other sleep related issues including hormone imbalances or emotional reasons. They can provide a more natural and holistic approach to treatment.

Two areas that are not often thought of or recognized as areas of concern in younger people that contribute to sleep issues include sleep apnea and hormonal imbalances. They can easily be dismissed as a non-issue for those under the age of 40 but they are becoming increasingly prevalent.

Jaw misalignment from past orthodontic work or the rise in xenoestrogens and endocrine disruptors in our environment can lie at the root of these concerns. You will probably need professional support for hormone imbalances or to get a sleep study done to see if there are other factors that are impacting your sleep. Your doctor or dentist can refer you to sleep study. Sleep apnea is far more prevalent than you think – and underlying factors may not be something you would consider an issue for you.

So let's chat about some easy but wonderful ways to support your sleep!

RESIRATORY ISSUES

Respiratory issues are a big concern that impact sleep quality. Different factors that play a role in respiratory issues and sleep include: allergies and mouth-breathing vs. nasal breathing. Continue reading below for tips on supporting your respiration related to these concerns.

Allergy Support: Allergies contribute to inflamed, blocked or narrower nasal structures which will affect your breathing. This will in in turn affect your sleep. Keep your room free of dust and regularly wash sheets and pillows. A humidifier can also help hydrate and soothe irritated and dry mucus membranes. Consider using a neti-pot to flush sinuses daily during allergy season. Nasal sprays that contain xylitol rather than medicated anti-histamines and corticosteroids are preferable for opening the airways.

There are homeopathic nasal sprays that can support the health of your sinuses and other homeopathic remedies that reduce allergy symptoms. Figure out what is contributing to allergy symptoms. Working with a homeopath can help your body become less reactive to allergens and reduce medication needs through boosting of the immune system. I have seen many clients go from needing daily Reactine or anti-histamine due to pet allergies or seasonal allergies to requiring only homeopathic remedies or nothing at all with a well prescribed homeopathic medicine.

> **Homeopathic Remedies for Allergies:**
> Homeocan carries two blends for allergies that I love. One is called Sinus and the other Allergy. If neither work, don't give up on homeopathy. It is very effective IF and WHEN the right remedies are given. You may require a homeopathic consult to get to the right remedy as finding the right one on your own is very difficult without training in the field!
> See Appendix A.

Liver Support: Your liver health needs to be supported when dealing with chronic allergies. See tenet #7.

Mouth breathing: Mouth breathing due to small jaw structure or past orthodontic work may also be contributing to respiratory issues which impacts sleep quality. Mouth breathing is problematic, contributing to inflammation, frequent waking, waking to use the washroom and many other health issues.

You may need to consider trying mouth tape for a few nights to see if that solves your issues (a simple fix!) and if that doesn't work it's probably time to see a holistic dentist or some other practitioner (e.g. chiropractor, osteopath or craniosacral therapist, myofunctional therapist) who will work with this issue. Before using mouth tape make sure you can breathe comfortably and easily through your nose! A myofunctional therapist can help you build strength in the muscles of the tongue, neck, throat and jaw as well as help with proper function so that you have better respiration.

SLEEP HYGIENE

Sleep Hygiene are routine recommendations that help promote quality sleep. These include: sleep in a dark, cool room, avoid screens 2 hours (including your phone!) or so before bed, keep a regular sleep schedule, have a bedtime routine and wind down at least 30 minutes before bed, dim your lights to improve melatonin production, disconnect from phone, tv or computer to reduce mental stimulation, try some relaxing techniques such as deep breathing, meditation or calming music, avoid caffeine in the afternoon, use your bed purely for sleep or sex, avoid late night intense physical activity, block out noise or use a white noise machine, use blackout curtains or an eye mask, take it easy with or avoid naps, avoid heavy foods before bed and avoid alcohol as it will interfere with your sleep. There are many other tips for improving sleep and you may need to figure out which works best for you as every person's needs are different.

SLEEP AIDS

- ➢ mouth tape – please use cautiously particularly if you suffer from sleep apnea and ensure you can breathe well through your nose!

- nasal spray (natural) to open airways – avoid corticosteroids if at all possible as they will eventually stop working effectively and can have nasty side effects
- nasal dilators or nasal strips
- sleep position (consider the pillow you use)
- air purifier (particularly for allergies or low air quality) or air humidifier (if air is super dry)
- black-out curtains or eye mask
- white noise machine

HORMONAL SUPPORT FOR SLEEP

Hormones have a significant impact on our sleep which is why peri-menopause and menopause can be such a difficult time of life for sleep. Try the following in conjunction with other sleep supports in this section.

Herbal teas: lemon balm, black cohosh, fennel, valerian, fenugreek

Essential oils in appropriate dosage and dilution can be applied to the bottoms of the feet and can be helpful hormone support: clary sage, geranium, lavender, basil

Homeopathic Hormonal Support: There are many other homeopathic options for hot flashes, palpitations, anxiety, insomnia and other hormonal issues so I'd **highly** recommend seeing a homeopath who can help with your specific needs and help your body transition to the hormonal changes in a much more natural way and reduce the symptoms and even eliminate them entirely. I have seen this work wonderfully for many women who have struggled with severe perimenopausal or menopausal symptoms. Consider doing an internet search for homeopathy for menopause to get remedy suggestions. Choose the remedy that has the closest description of your symptoms. The following listed are but a few of many that might be beneficial.

Homeopathic remedies that can be considered for support of the hormones include (but are not limited to):

- **Pulsatilla 30C** – a tendency to weepiness & often very attached to family. Changeable moods, irregular periods, lack of thirst and heat alternating with chill. Often feels better outdoors.
- **Calcarea Carbonica 30C** – may have heavy flood, flushing with chills, night sweats. Often has weight gain. Can feel quite anxious, fatigued but will continue to plug on, working hard.
- **Ignatia 30C** – lots of emotional ups and downs, feels very sensitive but hides this feeling and can become defensive; sudden outbursts of tears, lots of sighing. Can have headaches, irregular periods and muscle cramps.
- **Belladonna 30C** – hot flashes that occur with redness, congestion and profuse sweating

Dosing – 1-2 pellets as needed for symptoms up to 4 doses daily. If you find you need more doses to manage symptoms or need to take for longer than 2 weeks continuously it is recommended to see a homeopath.

EMOTIONAL/STRESS SLEEP SUPPORT

Calming our minds is essential to restful sleep. Often stress and anxiety build up during the day and when we finally relax at night they can 'hit' and it can be hard to know why. We can experience overthinking, restlessness, anxiety and all kinds of other mental and emotional symptoms. Cortisol, our stress hormone, should be lowest at night. However, with chronic stress, this hormone can be elevated at night which can make

you wakeful in the middle of the night. As such, managing our daytime stresses before bed is essential for improving sleep quality. A few ways in which to do this:
- Journalling before bed to destress and offload thoughts, stressors, anxieties
- talking with a loved ones about the things weighing on your mind,
- prayer,
- bible reading,
- avoiding stimulating tv shows/movies particularly 2-3 hours before bed
- reading books (not too stimulating!)
- listening to calming music
- deep breathing exercises

GENERAL SUPPORT FOR SLEEP

Turn off your WIFI/put your cellphone in airplane mode: The frequencies emitted by your WIFI and phone will disrupt your brain waves impacting your sleep.

Flower Essences: There are a few different options to help you emotionally depending on the exact issue affecting you. However, to cover your basis or try one, Bach Rescue Remedy Nighttime, is my #1 favourite support for anxiety/fear at night.

Magnesium: Magnesium glycinate or magnesium bisglycinate is a wonderful nervous system and muscle relaxant. Consider 1000-4000mg before bed if not medically contraindicated and to toleration.

Support your Circadian Rhythm: Don't underestimate the powerful effect of sunlight on good sleep. Ensuring you are getting morning sun (without sunglasses before 9am and even if it's overcast) and the dimming evening sun (after 4pm) is the best sleep medicine of all. It helps with the production of melatonin and helps set your circadian rhythm which in turn will affect your sleep quality. In addition, avoid screens 2-3 hours before bedtime, dimming the lights an hour before sleep and keeping a regular bedtime hour helps with setting a good circadian rhythm and supports natural production of melatonin, the hormone that impacts sleep.

Melatonin: Melatonin supplementation can also a wonderful option particularly for short periods of time but I would definitely try supporting a healthy circadian rhythm setting first. Melatonin can be supportive for sleep and has the additional benefit of being anti-viral and protective against breast cancers. You may need to play around with your dosage to see how you tolerate it. Don't be shy to dose high (up to 30mg a night) but I'd recommend starting low. I also would suggest that you don't depend on melatonin long-term if possible. Use it for short periods and wean off to see how your body's sleep rhythm is doing naturally. Melatonin production is impacted by age so it may help with sleep as you age.

Avoid Fluoride: Tap water contains fluoride and can contribute to hardening of the pineal gland which releases melatonin so avoid fluoridated water if you can.

Herbs: Obviously, there might come a time when you need additional sleep support. You really don't want to stay on supplements long-term so, in cases where you decide to use, remember the other sleep supports that you can use to help build a high-quality sleep cycle. *It is always best to seek*

professional support for sleep issues as there are often many factors to consider.
- ➢ 5-HTP can be helpful particularly if low mood is a struggle as well as sleep. 50-200mg can be taken 30 minutes before going to bed. Avoid if on SSRIs.
- ➢ L-Theanine 50-200mg 30-60 minutes before bed can help increase deep sleep.
- ➢ CBD, Kava Kava, St. John's Wort, Valerian and other herbs are considered as part of sleep support. Some of these do have contraindications so be sure to read the bottle and/or see a professional for further clarity.

Herbal Teas: Teas are a wonderful way to support sleep. Consider a cup of chamomile, Valerian tea, lavender, lemongrass, passionflower a few hours before bed (so you don't wake to use the toilet).

Essential Oils: Essential oils (diffused, sprayed, topically applied) such as lavender, chamomile, bergamot, cedarwood, sandalwood can create feelings of calm and relaxation.

Hot Shower or Bath: A hot shower or bath can help your body dump heat in response to the heat which in turn cools your core body temperature and helps you fall asleep.

Homeopathic Support: The best homeopathic medicine for sleep and stress is one prescribed by a homeopath as it will be specific to your concern which will in turn have the biggest impact on your sleep. Sleep can be affected by work stress, overthinking, earworms, anxiety related to various situations, overfatigue and more. Homeopathic medicines can be chosen that have direct impact on specific situational issues which then produce the best results emotionally, mentally and physically.

General homeopathic blends/brands for sleep: Dr. Reckeweg #14, Boiron's Quietude, Homeocan's Insomnia and/or Stress, Orange Natural's Stress & Calm. There are many other brands that carry homeopathic sleep blends. Each brand/blend contain different remedies so if one doesn't seem to work try another one with a few different ingredients! Dosing is usually on the label but you can always take homeopathic remedies in the middle of the night if awake as well to help you calm down and return to sleep.

CHINESE BODY CLOCK & ORGAN AFFINITY

In Chinese medicine waking at specific times during the night is indicative of certain organs or emotions needing some extra loving care and attention. This is more specific to when you find yourself waking at the same time of night regularly. Based on that you can take into consideration what kind of support is necessary, whether it is physical or emotional.

You can consider a variety of herbal teas, tinctures, homeopathic remedies for organ support and strengthening, but also pay attention to the specific emotions tied to that time period as well for improving sleep as your emotions play a large role in sleep as well.

- **9-11pm:** time of the endocrine system when the body is brought back into balance and your enzymes are replenished. It is recommended to sleep at this time so the body can conserve energy for the following day. Feelings of paranoia or confusion may also be felt.
- **11pm-1am:** time of the Gall Bladder which has a close relationship to the liver.
  - The gallbladder is associated with feelings of bitterness.

- **1-3am:** time of the Liver which plays a role in many bodily functions including cleansing and creating new blood. Waking at this time could indicated some weakness with your liver or detoxification pathways.
    - The liver is associated with feelings of anger.
    - Note: this time is also associated with a spike in cortisol (our stress hormone) so addressing stress in addition to liver health may need to be considered.
- **3-5am:** the time of the Lungs and when the lungs are detoxed
    - The lungs are also associated with feelings of grief and sadness and emotional worry.
- **5-7am:** the time of the large intestine. Unsurprisingly this is the ideal time for a large bowel movement.
    - The large intestine is associated with feelings of guilt.

MANAGING BLOOD SUGAR IMBALANCE

Blood sugar imbalances can affect sleep and can cause waking at night. If you do not have a diagnosed blood sugar imbalance but suffer with waking from hunger or random waking between 1am-3am blood sugar imbalance could be a contributing factor. Address blood sugar issues with the help of a naturopath, nutritionist or functional doctor. Supporting your liver health is a good place to start (see Tenet #7). A handful of nuts or seeds before bed can help keep blood sugar from dropping too low overnight.

Tenet #4: Minerals

I mentioned minerals previously in the water section but I'd like to briefly talk about how essential they are to health. Most of us are minerally deficient due to poor diet, chronic digestive issues, poor water quality, high intake of processed foods, chronic stress, on-going health issues, high levels of toxicity in our environments and because food is often picked too early. Fruits and veggies get an injection of nutrients when they ripen on the vine and most of our food is picked to early so it will be ripe when it arrives at the grocery store.

Minerals play a role in hormone creation, cellular function, enzymatic reactions, blood sugar balance, nervous system function, immune strength and much more.

When considering taking any type of mineral supplement remember that most are synthetically made in a lab. It is far superior to naturally source minerals as they are more easily absorbed and bio-available.

Different seasons of life call for different needs and amount of minerals. If you are trying to get pregnant, are pregnant or breast-feeding you will need more minerals to nourish your body.

SUPPORTING MINERAL BALANCE

High quality salt: Adding a high-quality salt to your diet (not iodized!) is a wonderful way to increase your mineral intake. I love Redmond Sea Salt and either adding it to a bottle of water or just tossing it into my mouth direct and drinking with a sip of water. Most of us are actually salt deficient due to all the cautions around ingesting salt. Remember that natural sea salts or other high-quality salt are actually beneficial to the body.

Animal meat/organs: Animal organs and meat are some of the most nutrient and mineral dense foods. They are easily absorbable and if you don't like animal organs you can easily access dehydrated versions in pill form. See Appendix A for Brand Suggestions & Discount Codes. These supplements are safe for adults and kids (dose dependent) and the pills can be opened and added to a smoothie, meatballs or other meal.

Tissue salts: Tissue salts are homeopathic and consist of 12 different mineral compounds that can support mineral imbalances in the body and stimulate the body to heal itself. They can be used regularly and can be tailored to specific conditions or health needs. They often come as single salts or in various combinations for specific needs.

Supplements: Shilajit or Humic-Fulvic Acid Complex is a way of supporting mineral balance. Both have their unique benefits – for example, shilajit is a wonderful hormonal support. Finding a quality provider of these can be difficult so do your research. See Appendix A.

Tenet #5: Nervous System Retraining & Health

Healing your nervous system is a must for a healthy body. Unfortunately, many of us live with a higher state of stress than is good for us. Stress that leads to poor health outcomes can be compounded by underlying long-term poor adaptive stress response due to childhood issues, trauma, etc. For healing we need to support and heal the nervous system.

We need to rewire how our body has learned to respond to stressful and even non-stressful life events. Although there are a lot of programs available that take you through emotional healing and somatic exercises as part of nervous system retraining, you have been given many different healing exercises as you worked through the previous sections of this book on emotions and trauma. Whether you wish to invest further in this area is up to you.

I'd like to spend a bit of time to explain what happens in your brain when trauma occurs so you can understand why you might be triggered by certain visuals, lights, sounds or smells.

Our brains are wired to process our life experiences through the frontal lobe of our brain which is responsible for calm decision-making. When severe trauma occurs, rather than the experience being processed through the calm, rational frontal lobe, it gets rerouted through the amygdala, where fear is processed. When our amygdala processes the information, it is not stored as a cohesive memory but rather in fragments of sensory information such as lights, sounds or certain smells, and then that memory is then stored in those fragments. This is why you might find a certain smells, sounds or lights can trigger a fight, freeze, flight response.

Our brains can become hardwired to processing normal, non-threatening life events through the amygdala due to inherited trauma, unprocessed/unhealed negative childhood events and chronic stress. This is a problem when we want to heal as the body is stuck in protective mode.

When we want to heal this trauma, we need to rewire the brain and move our processing and storing of experiences (traumatic or not), from the amygdala to the frontal lobe again. We must learn to attend to the vagus nerve which plays a role in the health of our brain, gut and heart. Simultaneously we also need to heal the gut so that we feed good information to the brain from the gut via the vagus nerve. This takes time and patience.

Our bodies are largely electrical, sending signals electrically, communicating needs, emotions, experiences and more with electrical signals. Electrical signals require healthy routes on which to travel (through fascia, the vagus nerve, etc.) and require adequate amounts of minerals to send those signals. This is why we need to attend to the physical aspects (like ingesting minerals, attending to the fascia, healing the gut) and the emotional/mental (working through trauma, supporting our mental/emotional health).

Our thoughts have an immense impact on our overall health as we discussed in the sections on identity, emotions and trauma. Trauma has powerful impact on our subconscious inner dialogue – "I'm broken, I'm a burden" – so this is why time has been invested in previous sections working through the way you think and talk about yourself and why emotional health and healing from past trauma plays a pivotal role in your physical healing.

If there is deep nervous system (NS) dysregulation that you have found is not responding to the healing exercises or when you attend to your emotional needs, working with a therapist is highly recommended. They can use their expertise to tailor exercises to your needs and can help you identify where you may need additional emotional support.

The majority of us will benefit from practicing the healing exercises discussed in previous sections. I have also included some recommendations in Appendix A. If you haven't yet invested in learning or practicing any of the recommended exercises now is the time to go back and learn them. Some of these included practices such as life-giving identity affirmations, grounding, breathing exercises, rest, meditation (scripture), prayer, journalling, movement, getting creative and more.

Lastly, do *not* underestimate the power of rest. Rest when you need to and rest as a regular life discipline. A constantly stressed body will not heal.

Below I will share some information on natural health supplements to support the nervous system. They are useful alongside the healing exercises and provide an extra level of support when you are healing.

SUPPORTS FOR NERVOUS SYSTEM HEALTH

Sleep: Sleep is essential for supporting a healthy nervous system. Aim for 7-9 hours a night if possible.

Digestive Health & Diet: Diet and gut health play a fundamental role in your nervous system health. Eating a diet rich in various fresh fruits and vegetables, meats and other sources of proteins, complex carbohydrates and healthy fats is great, providing minerals, nutrients and other essential amino acids. Variety is key here. Include foods rich in omega-3 fatty acids such as walnuts, flaxseeds, chia seeds, sardines, salmon, brussels sprouts, cauliflower and spinach.

Minerals: see Tenet #4

Exercise & Movement: See Tenet #8

Adaptogenic Herbs: Adaptogenic herbs help support the body to function well particularly when undergoing stress. When in a constant state of stress or nervous system dysfunction you can end up physically exhausted and needing more sleep than usual. Taking adaptogens have benefits such as improving energy, concentration, sleep, regulating body systems and more. such as: rhodiola, ginseng, holy basil, ashwagandha, astragalus root, licorice root, schisandra, maca, shilijat and mushrooms (reishi, cordyceps) to name just a few. There are many different blends of adaptogens available or you can take them individually. See Appendix A.

Herbal teas: valerian, chamomile, lavender, green tea, peppermint, passionflower

Rest & Disconnect: Need a I say more? Schedule it in as a regular practice. Do nothing or do something creative. Do something you enjoy. Disconnect from social media.

Gratefulness: Make a list of 5 things you are thankful for. This will lift your mood and change your mindset.

Get into nature: See Tenet #9

Epsom salts baths: with lavender or other calming essential oils will help calm the nervous system.

Essential oils: Diffuse essential oils such as a citrus oil (boosts mood), lavender, peppermint, ginger or another smell that you enjoy.

Magnesium: No surprise here again. Magnesium bis-glycinate/glycinate is calming to the nervous system and helps relax muscular tension. Magnesium L-threonate is also one to consider for brain health. Feel free to take a combo of both.

Cold baths: this can cause your parasympathetic nervous system (the one that helps you relax) to kick in. If you don't have access to a full ice bath you can try various cold water immersion by dunking your face in an ice bath or applying a cold compress to your chest or back of the neck.

Homeopathic medicines: Homeopathics are my favourite way to support the nervous system and do a wonderful job in bringing calm in so many different situations from public speaking, chronic stress, work stress, relational stress, financial stress and more. A well prescribed homeopathic medicine will not only help calm you but will actually support your immune system, mood and mental health. Information on where to purchase the following can be found in Appendix A.

- **Bach Flower Rescue Remedy:** My favourite, effective go-to for stress and anxiety relief would be Rescue Remedy. It is an incredible support in times of stress, fear and anxiety. There is even a night-time version. I have heard from many clients that it is as effective as pharmaceutical medications for managing anxiety. It does not interfere with medications. It comes in a variety of forms (sprays, drops, gum and pills).
- **Other homeopathics** that I highly recommend for high anxiety situations would be a blend of Arsenicum Album, Aconitum Napellus & Argentum Nitricum in a 200C. You can take 2 pellets up to 6x daily. See a professional homeopath if you need to use this regularly as a more individualized remedy or different potency will get you better results.
- There are a variety of nervous system support blends from companies such as Pascoe (Zincum similiaplex), Homeocan (Stress), Boiron (Quietude, Acidum Phosphoricum Compose, Passiflora Compose) and Dr. Reckeweg (R#184).

Tenet #6: Tend to your Gut

Unsurprisingly, your digestive system is an essential piece of your wellness and it is often referred to as your second brain. Your gut impacts your ability to absorb nutrients, make neurotransmitters (for sleep, mood, etc.), plays a role in immune function, affects your weight, eliminates toxins and impacts your overall wellness particularly. We discussed the nervous system in Tenet #5 and so you understand that your digestive health plays a significant role in your nervous system. Poor gut health contributes to chronic inflammation and emotional distress/illness, food sensitivities, gas/bloating/diarrhea and much more.

Gut motility is important and at a fundamental level we need to address issues of drainage if you struggle with any type of digestive motility issue (diarrhea, constipation, heartburn, etc.). See Tenet #7 to learn more about optimizing drainage and detoxification of your digestive system. <u>If you cannot excrete toxins well (think constipation) or absorb nutrients (think chronic diarrhea, gastritis, food sensitivities) properly this will contribute to many kinds of health issues and underlying inflammation.</u> In addition, an unhealthy gut often means an imbalanced microbiome where bacteria, fungi and parasites can wreak havoc on your digestive, emotional, mental, immune and overall health. There has been more research into the role that parasites play in the development of diseases such as Parkinson's and Multiple Sclerosis so you can see that your gut health is foundational to overall wellness.

Remember that the emotions you experience impact the health of your gut and the opposite is true. If you are not dealing with your emotions your gut won't heal and your health will continue to decline and stagnate. Alternatively, if you do not take care of your digestive health your mood, energy, brain health and more will be negatively affected. Having previously discussed the role of the vagus nerve in the communication between the gut and the brain it not surprising that supporting and building resiliency of your nervous system is an essential piece of the picture. See Tenet #9 and the Healing Exercises throughout this book to build strength in this area.

Below are some tips on supporting a healthy microbiome, building gut health and healing your digestive system. As usual, this does not replace medical advice and caution should be taken in on any medications or struggle with any specific digestive related health conditions.

SUPPORT FOR GUT HEALTH & HEALING

Kickstart your digestion: Aside from using bitters, start your day with a full glass of warm (as warm as you can handle) water with some lemon or organic apple cider vinegar to kickstart digestion.

Bitters: Consider adding bitters to your diet every day which can stimulate digestion, help balance blood sugar, reduce sugar cravings and reduce indigestion, gas and bloating. Bitters enhance the production of bile which is essential to good digestion. Bitters typically come as herbal drops but leafy greens and triphala are other options.

Digestive enzymes: I wouldn't generally recommend routine intake of digestive enzymes unless you require them for a specific issue. Chronic digestive issues such as indigestion, heartburn, diarrhea, constipation, and/or IBS are better treated with a holistic approach that addresses the underlying cause rather than treating the symptoms.

Address Motility: Motility issues like constipation, diarrhea, indigestion, and irritable bowel can be addressed through incorporating regular drainage protocols (see Tenet #7), ensuring you chew your food well, have adequate water and fiber intake and healing your gut through a diet that avoids foods that you are sensitive to and with appropriate supplementation.

Abdominal massage is a wonderful way to support your digestion. Starting in the Right Lower Quadrant of your abdomen (by R hip bone) gently massage in circles with fingers slowly moving upwards to your ribs, then moving across your abdomen to your Left side under the ribs and then downward towards your Left hipbone.

Increase gut microbiome biodiversity through gardening, getting your hands into soil regularly, deep breathing in natural environments (you inhale tiny amounts of dirt).

Walking/Movement: Take a slow walk or gently move your body after eating to stimulate digestion, reduce gas and bloating after eating.

Fiber: Fiber is an essential for good digestive function, detoxification and more. It promotes a healthy microbiome and it helps rid the body of toxins. However, if you eat a lot of fiber and find yourself gassy this is often due to too high fiber intake. Reduce intake and see how the body responds.

Fats: Healthy fats are essential to hormone production. Healthy fats include olive oil, ghee, butter, tallow and coconut oil. Seed oils are best avoided if possible as they are very inflammatory. Nuts are a great source of fat but they can be irritating to the digestive system. Remember that oils and nuts will go rancid so consider refrigerating or freezing nuts and specific oils. Different oils also have different points at which they degrade. As such, be intentional to use certain oils unheated and cook with specific oils. For example, Extra Virgin or Unrefined Coconut Oil, Extra Virgin Olive Oil and butter have lower smoke points so they should be avoided when cooking over temperatures of 350 degrees Fahrenheit.

Intentionality: Eat slowly, chew your food well, eat sitting down and avoid stressful conversations or social media while eating.

Water: Ensure you are drinking enough water to support good digestion. Not ingesting enough water contributes to sluggish digestion and constipation.

Diversify your diet: Eating a variety of fruits and vegetables contributes to an increasingly diverse microbiome.

Probiotics: Probiotic foods can be ingested to support bowel health. Eating probiotic foods is generally the best way to diversify your gut microbiome and repopulate it effectively. Typically, probiotic supplements only affect the gut while you are taking them. Probiotic foods include: yogurts, kefirs, kombuchas, sauerkraut, etc. Remember that these can rapidly impact your digestion and cause diarrhea or loose stool if eating too much at a time. Be slow when introducing probiotic foods and see how your body responds. Eating a diet rich in various types of fruits and vegetables promotes a more diverse microbiome which contributes to overall health.
o   Probiotic supplements may be helpful with specific health issues and are often required in cases where antibiotic use has occurred. However, given that there are many brands and a variety of different strains it is often best to get a probiotic prescribed by a qualified practitioner as many brands do not have sufficient research showing their benefits. They also can cause more issues if you suffer from chronic digestive issues.

Note - There is quite a large body of evidence stating that ingestion of Saccharomyces boulardii is beneficial in cases when antibiotics are taken.

Stress management: Stress can cause indigestion, reflux, constipation, diarrhea and much more. See Tenet #9 and 10 to address this if this is a concern.

Avoid Alcohol: Unfortunately, there is never a healthy amount or good time of day to ingest alcohol. It is highly inflammatory, impacts sleep and mood. Consider reducing or avoiding entirely.

Food sensitivities: Avoid foods that you are sensitive to until you have healed your gut. Food sensitivities are tied to gut health. If you have them, you can typically heal them with appropriate care.

Elimination Diets & Food Sensitivity Testing: An elimination diet is worth considering for uncovering and healing food sensitivities. Common food sensitivities include: wheat, corn, dairy, gluten, soy. More information on how to do an elimination diet can be found online. These protocols take work but can save you quite a bit of money compared to doing food sensitivity testing. Food sensitivity testing can be done bio-energetically, via blood sample or through a medical allergist/immunologist. I have always liked the simplicity of bio-energetic testing through a nutritionist if you do decide to spend the money. Testing can save you a lot of time and energy rather than doing the hard work of an elimination diet.

Avoid Glyphosate: Much of the food we eat has been sprayed with glyphosate (roundup) and this herbicide wreaks havoc on the gut. Many people with gluten sensitivity actually are dealing with glyphosate toxicity. Supporting your liver is necessary for the body as it eliminates glyphosate. However, avoiding foods high in glyphosate is essential. In Canada these foods include: wheat, barley, oats, chickpeas, flax, lentils, mustard, dry beans, canola, peas, soybeans and faba beans. Glyphosate can be detoxed with homeopathic remedies available through some homeopathic practitioners.

Fasting: Fasting is a hot topic which I won't get into depth here due to the highly individualized needs of people. Some people do well with intermittent fasting and others do not. I will say that as a general principle, for women in their childbearing years, intermittent fasting can have negative impact on hormone health due to the lower caloric intake which can in turn reduce fertility.

Herbal Teas: Anise seed, Fennel, Licorice, peppermint, Slippery Elm, Ginger

Get Professional Support: Consider seeing a qualified Homeopath, Acupuncturist, Chinese Medicine Doctor, Nutritionist, Naturopath for specialized gut healing protocols particularly if it is a long-term issue or you take medications for digestive issues. These practitioners all play a different role in healing, some focusing more on supplements and diets (more often the naturopath, nutritionist), while others may be more focused on addressing the emotional and personal pieces that impact digestive health (typically a homeopath). A Chinese Medicine Doctor, Acupuncturist and Homeopath will also look at the energetic imbalance in the body and seek to bring that into alignment.

NATURAL SUPPLEMENTS FOR GUT HEALTH

Below are a few recommendations for homeopathics and supplements that can help with digestive health. Recognize that these are limited and not specific to specialized needs. As always see a specialist or doctor before begin any protocols or implementing any tips if you have health concerns or take any medications. Google is also a wonderful resource for learning more about which homeopathic remedies can be helpful for specific issues.

*Recommended homeopathic dosing for acute issues is 2 pellets of 30C dissolved in the mouth away from food/mint/coffee by 15-30 minutes. They can be taken every 30 minutes up to 3x for relief. They will not interfere with medications. However, if you need to take these long-term it is best to work with a professional to determine the underlying issue.

Constipation: If constipation is a chronic issue this needs to be addressed by a qualified health practitioner as the digestive route needs to be open for drainage and detoxification of toxins. *Utilizing supplements or herbs long term to keep the bowels regular indicates imbalance that requires professional support.*
- Supplement: Orange Naturals Constipation, Triphala, Senna Tea, Magnesium Citrate

Indigestion and/or heartburn: Chronic heartburn or indigestion is often treated with medications that reduce acidity. However, it is often that there is low stomach acid which is why you will get heartburn. Medications and low acidity also contribute to reduced nutrient uptake so long-term indigestion should be addressed with a natural health professional as you will need more support to provide your body with lost nutrients and vitamins as well as heal from this chronic issue.

For infrequent heartburn or indigestion consider the following support:
- ½ tbsp apple cider vinegar or lemon juice in a little water after a meal (if this is painful or uncomfortable you may be dealing with an ulcer)
- eat an apple or apple sauce
- Homeopathic remedies including Arsenicum Album, Carbo vegetalis, Lycopodium or Nux Vomica in a 6C or 30C potency. You can take 1-2 pellets after a meal, every 15-30 minutes until there is relief (maximum total of 4 doses).
- Homeopathic blends for digestion are worth considering. They work quickly and are completely natural. Brands: Homeocan, Orange Naturals
- Teas can also be taken to improve digestion such as peppermint, fennel, licorice, ginger, anise seed.

For healing gastritis or a chronically inflamed digestive system: ** Note: due to the chronic nature of this issue it is best to work with a health professional for healing this problem.
- Supplements such as slippery elm, L-Glutamine, licorice root, peppermint can be calming and healing to the digestive system.
- Homeopathic remedies including Arsenicum Album, Carbo vegetalis, Lycopodium in a 6C or 30C potency. You can take 1-2 pellets after a meal, every 15-30 minutes until there is relief (maximum total of 4 doses).

Tenet #7: Drainage & Cellular Optimization

Drainage is one of the most foundational pieces to good health and is certainly needed in our increasingly toxic world.

We often think of drainage as a form of detoxification but it is a lot more than that! Yes, it includes sweating, pooping, peeing, and breathing to rid the body of waste and toxins, but it is also the movement of wastes at a cellular level. It involves whole systems (lymphatic system, respiratory, digestive, circulatory etc.), the organs (liver, lungs, heart, kidneys) and each individual cell.

If you consider how the organs and body systems remove the garbage from your body at the 'larger' level, *cellular drainage is about increasing the health and metabolic potential of the cell at the microscopic level which is needed for the organ and other systems to function at their best. Simply, supporting drainage optimizes cellular function.* When you support cellular drainage, the organs and systems in your body are better able to produce and regulate hormones, regulate blood sugar, detoxify the body's waste and toxins, digest food and nutrients, filter the blood, increasing energy and boost immune function to name just a few benefits.

> **How often should I do a drainage protocol?**
> The majority of us could benefit from an organ drainage protocol at some point during the year, if not on a regular basis, depending on the health issues you live with or due to the environments you live and work in.
> If your health issues are specific to certain organs or body systems then consider doing a more specific kind of drainage related to that organ.

Impaired cellular function within the organs affects inflammation, energy, focus and concentration, digestion, circulation, breathing and every possible level of our ability to function. Cellular energy is vital to good health!

The following list of symptoms related to poor drainage is incomplete but hopefully includes symptoms that you might not have thought related to poor organ drainage. Although these symptoms may not be directly caused by poor drainage, it can contribute to the problem.

> **Symptoms of Poor Drainage:** constipation, irregular bowel habits, skin issues of any kind (acne, eczema, rashes, etc.), sluggish digestion, brain fog, nausea on waking in the morning, chronic inflammation, liver cirrhosis, kidney stones, gallstones, gallbladder issues, hormonal issues or imbalances, seasonal allergies, recurrent infections, inability to eat in the morning, undereye circles, chronic fatigue, joint pain, muscle pain and more.

Some of my favourite effective and affordable drainage supplements are herbal teas and homeopathic remedies. I really like homeopathic drainage protocols because they are safe for all ages, safe to use alongside medications, and they are gentle on the body. They also are capable of strengthening weakened organs and can be taken with herbs which can enhance the effect of the herb on the organ you are optimizing.

If you have any health issues or are taking medication, please use caution and consider working with a trained health practitioner who can recommend what is safe for you to take. Consider utilizing homeopathics instead as they will be much better tolerated.

A homeopath can help you determine which blends are best for you and don't be afraid to ask at your local health food store or search google if you have no idea where to start. I hope the following list will provide some basic guidelines for you to begin your drainage protocol. You will see some of my favourite drainage remedies or brands but again, this is not a complete list so don't be afraid to use another brand. Both the homeopathic and herbal blends can be purchased at health food stores or you can find more on purchasing them online in Appendix A.

REMINDER: Drinking plenty of natural or structured water supports drainage and helps cellular function.

WHERE TO BEGIN YOUR DRAINAGE JOURNEY: HOMEOPATHY

I typically recommend use of General Homeopathics below as a safe starting point as the other types of homeopathic drainage tend to need professional guidance.

There are different types of drainage blends in homeopathic medicine. <u>Working with a practitioner will give you the best results</u> but you can use google or visit a health food store to get some guidance.

> For chronic disease and complex health issues I'd always recommend working with a homeopathic or naturopathic practitioner as you do not wish to aggravate your health issues further. If you take any medications, working with a practitioner is highly recommended as certain supplements can interfere or cause a reaction.

You will need to do some research to point you to which type of homeopathic drainage and which blend is specific to your condition and the organ you are supporting.

Consider what your aim or goal is – strengthening, balancing or healing of the organ.

- **Organotherapy:** these remedies are made from healthy organ extracts or organ secretions; these can be used to heal, strengthen and balance an organ's production of substances they produce such as hormones
  - Brands: Genestra (HAD, HFE, HHR, HLIP, HKI, HLU, HPNP, HTPT, HTYP, HTHY), Life Choice

- **Oligotherapy:** remedies made from trace elements such as metals and metalloids that are naturally present in the human body in minute quantities and are necessary for normal metabolic functioning; typically used when the organ is functioning well for extra support during stressful periods
  - Brands: UNDA

- **Phytotherapy and Gemmotherapy:** made from plant extracts or bud extracts, these are the basic elements to use for the drainage of all chronic diseases. They must be used for prolonged courses of treatment, usually for a minimum of 2 months each.
  - Brands: Boiron, Homeocan, HerbalGem, UNDA & Genestra

- **General Homeopathics:** often made from a plant, homeopathic blends can be a gentle stimulus to the organ it has an affinity for. For example, *carduus marianus* 6X is the homeopathic version of milk thistle which has an affinity to the liver and gallbladder.

o Brands: Pascoe, Dr. Reckeweg, UNDA, St. Francis Herb Farm, Martin & Pleasance

Herbal Tinctures:
Herbal tinctures are a wonderful way to take herbs specific to health conditions and/or organs. Herbal tinctures are generally made with alcohol as a preservative. These contain measurable amounts of plants extracts and they can be too stimulating for some people.

Caution: <u>You probably want to start with a homeopathic support before going this direction if you suffer from</u>: a chronic health issue(s), have symptoms of poor drainage (see above for list), have diseased organs and/or you are sensitive to plants/herbs/medications.

Brands that I like (but not limited to) include: (see Appendix A for purchasing options)
- Genestra
- Natural Factors
- Orange Naturals
- NewRoots
- St. Francis Herbal Farm

> **Remember that it is always better to start drainage gently and you can add herbal tinctures in later. In fact, you may want to try herbal teas or homeopathic options before integrating a herbal tincture.**

Herbal Teas:
Herbal teas can be chosen in various forms including as a combination of herbs so they can drain several organs and body

systems, or they can be taken solo, chosen based on which organ or body system needing support.

Many herbs found in tea can be used in homeopathic form for the same issues. For example, carduus marianus 6X can be taken for liver and gallbladder issues. It is commonly known as Milk Thistle and can easily be found as a tea. You can even take them both as a tea and in a homeopathic remedy (use a lower potency such as 3x, 6x, 12x) for organ support and healing.

Try to purchase organic herbal teas.

CAUTION: Be aware that certain herbs may be contraindicated during pregnancy or breastfeeding or with certain medical issues. Some may also interact with specific medications. Be sure to do your research or get professional support before taking any herbs.

> *If starting a new herb and you have long-standing health issues I'd recommend first looking at homeopathic support as it is the most gentle and safe, then consider adding in a tea.*
>
> *Using herbal tinctures is generally my last recommendation unless advised by a health practitioner.***

Teas/herbs with their organ affinity (this is not an exhaustive list):
- ➢ **Liver & Gallbladder:** Dandelion, Milk Thistle, Burdock, Sencha Green, Yerba Mate, Turmeric, Parsley, Cilantro, Pau D'arco, Rosemary
- ➢ **Kidneys & Bladder:** Bearberry, Cornsilk, Horsetail, Parsley, Cilantro, Green tea, Nettle, Alfalfa, Juniper, Uva

Ursi, Turmeric, Burdock, Ashwaganda Root, Marshmallow root
- **Lymph:** Red Clover, Burdock, Cleavers, Calendula, Goldenseal, Astragalus, Echinacea, Ginger, Garlic
- **Lungs:** Yarrow, Licorice, Stinging nettle, Horehound, Mullein, Ginseng, Elderberry, Eucalyptus, Thyme, Oregano, Rosemary, Astragalus Root, Marshmallow root
- **Heart:** Astragalus Root, Lemongrass, Hawthorn, Green, Olive Leaf, Hibiscus, Garlic, Ginseng, Cinnamon, Fenugreek, Pau D'arco
- **Spleen:** ginger, dandelion root, chamomile tea, peppermint tea, green tea, licorice root
- **Uterus:** Nettle, Red Raspberry Leaf, Black Cohosh, Moringa Leaf, Vitex (chasteberry), Dong Quai, Red Clover
    - *Note: if pregnant or breastfeeding some of these herbs may be contraindicated*
- **Skin:** nettle, oatstraw, oregon grape, matcha and the liver teas (see above)
- **Brain:** Ginseng, Rosemary, Green, Ginger, Gingko Bilboa
- **Blood:** Garlic, Cilantro, Rooibos, Nettle, the Liver teas (see above)
- **Stomach:** Anise seed, Slippery Elm

Lymphatic Drainage:

Do not forget to add a lymphatic drainage routine as a regular part of your daily life. The lymphatic system is a waste removal system and often gets neglected in favour of taking tinctures, herbs and other supplements. Draining the lymph system has many positive results including stimulating the immune system, reducing swelling, improving skin conditions and circulation and more.

Tattoos, tight clothes and inactivity can hinder lymphatic drainage so take special care to incorporate draining the lymph particularly if those describe your situation. There are many simple ways to practice lymphatic massage including gentle massage to specific points on the body (called termini) , dry brushing, jumping up and down and using a vibration plate. There are also many videos on YouTube showing how to do lymphatic massage if you have no idea where to start. Lastly, remember that lymphatic massage is *gentle*; more pressure is not better in this situation.

Castor Oil Packs:
These can be a wonderful way to support drainage. Castor oil packs are used externally on the body, placed over the specific organ needing extra support or drainage. Be sure to use organic, hexane-free, cold pressed castor oil. You do not need to add external heat as your body will warm it up. There are many protocols on-line for using castor oil packs on different parts of the body. Again, consulting a health professional before using may be worth considering. Avoid using during pregnancy and during your menstrual cycle if you have a heavy menses.

CAUTION: When dealing with lymphedema or other underlying health conditions you should receive training on how to do this correctly.

> **Basic Instructions for castor oil pack for liver drainage:**
> You will need: a high-quality organic castor oil, an old towel or flannel. Old clothing is helpful to wear as the oil will stain your clothing. Initially apply quarter-sized amount of organic castor oil to your abdomen, including over the liver area. Fold the towel or flannel and use it to cover your abdomen. Sometimes a piece of plastic or a large belt of some kind may be used to hold it in place. Rest for 30-60 minutes and allow the oil to work its magic. Some people sleep with the pack on (just beware that it will stain your pjs and sheets!). When you have finished you can fold the flannel and keep wrapped in a container for use later. For later use you can reuse the flannel but you may need to reapply the oil. Either let the oil absorb into the skin or wash off.
>
> Recommended use of a castor oil pack is different on needs but general use is at least four consecutive days per week for one month for optimal results.

Methylene Blue (MB):

MB is a compound that is used to improve mitochondrial function which is the source of energy within the cell. The mitochondria effects overall energy and cellular function. It is a potent antioxidant and antiviral and there are many studies showing its efficacy particularly as a neuroprotective compound. Any disease process that is associated with poor energy may benefit from MB use including chronic fatigue syndrome, heart disease, dementia, cancer as well as depression, stroke, cerebral ischemia, Alzheimer's, traumatic brain injury, Parkinson's disease, chronic infections, viral and fungal infections and more ((PMID 28840449).

It has been shown to have anti-aging effects as well and can be applied topically (it will stain!) for conditions such as psoriasis. It has been shown to boost collagen production. I have made my own skin blend by mixing MB with tallow butter (from fatskn©) for a lovely face cream.

By improving the cells' energy, it can promote faster recovery in simple cases of cold and flu and other viral infections.

Information on purchasing pharmaceutical grade MB can be found in Appendix A.

Note: Expect to pee blue.

> CAUTION: **Methylene blue should be considered with the help of a qualified medical practitioner.** Although it has been around for decades and is fairly safe to consume **AVOID taking if you are taking SSRIs, tricyclic antidepressants, MAOIs, certain pain drugs, St. John's wort, Ginseng, cold and allergy medications, amphetamines, blood pressure drugs, some antibiotics/antifungals, recreational drugs, Tegretol, disulphiram, certain pain drugs.** In addition, avoid foods that contain tyramine (cheese, soy sauce, liver, alcohol and salami) while using.

Antioxidants:

Antioxidants in the form of fresh fruits and vegetables or supplements are highly recommended for their beneficial health protectant qualities. Not only do they support your body to detoxify due to the regular exposure to toxins in our world, they help prevent cancer, boost cellular energy and function and reduce development of chronic disease. Eat a diet rich in fruit and vegetables (the more different the colours the better!) and

varied in proteins such as fish, eggs and other meats. Ingest organic foods if possible.
- ➢ **Vitamin C** – you can add this in but if you eat a diet rich in red/orange/yellow colour foods you will be ingesting this vitamin
- ➢ **Vitamin E** – legumes, almonds, avocado are a few natural sources. You can also supplement this as well. Lifeblud.co has a wonderful high quality Vitamin E in pill or drop form that is seed-oil free (REVIVE for 10% off)

Grounding, Homeopathy & Other Energy Therapies:

The frequencies emitted by the earth as well as sunlight, drinking and bathing in structured water and sound frequencies have the power to influence cells to optimize their function. Electromagnetic frequencies have the power to increase cellular energy and function in both positive and negative ways. Homeopathic medicines, when prescribed by a qualified practitioner, take into consideration your overall function (mental, emotional, physical) and a well prescribed remedy supports cellular function and drainage evidenced by an improvement in sleep, energy and overall wellness. See Tenet #9 to learn more about other energy therapies that can be used to support organ drainage and assist in optimizing cellular function.

Tenet # 8: Mobility & Strength

Not much needs to be said on the importance of mobility and strength in your health. Exercise and mobility can affect the following: organ drainage.

- mood
- blood sugar regulation
- stress tolerance
- life expectancy
- pain levels
- bone density
- weight management
- sleep quality
- energy levels
- brain function
- sexual health

INTEGRATING MOVEMENT WHEN LIVING WITH CHRONIC PAIN

Given that many you reading this book struggle with physical health issues, you may wonder how or if you can safely incorporate exercise into your daily life and where to even begin. Movement is essential for pain management and pain can be drastically reduced with increased movement, flexibility and strength.

To begin, I would highly recommend to *just start moving* every day even if it's gentle stretching and range of motion exercises (putting a joint through its full range of motion either passively or actively) on the bed or a chair. Walking slowly, even for short periods of time is beneficial. Take the stairs when you normally would take the elevator. Swimming and biking are wonderful low impact workouts. Again, you do not need to have high resistance. The point is to just *move*.

There may be an in-between period where you may wonder if you are making things worse as stiffness and pain can occur when you start moving or when you begin building muscle. You will need to learn what is 'good' pain and 'bad' pain. This is why it is important to pay attention to your body. New pain is not necessarily bad pain. This is an important principle.

Take the time to recover between sessions if you aren't certain what is good or bad pain. If you don't even know where to start or you are afraid, consider working with a fitness professional who will work with your limitations. There are also many YouTube videos that are specific for health issues.

CARDIOVASCULAR HEALTH, FLEXIBILITY & STRENGTH TRAINING

In the past there has been a strong emphasis on cardiovascular health as the reason for exercise. However, for the best physical health outcomes there needs to be a focus on a combination of cardiovascular exercise, strength training and flexibility. All are essential to health and wellness and should be implemented in some way. Stiffness and weakness are huge contributors to musculoskeletal pain and are often confused with pain from the disease process itself. This is why taking it slow and working with a professional can be helpful in discerning how your body responds and tailoring to your specific needs.

Weights are a wonderful addition to an exercise regimen. You can use canned veggies as weights or buy weights. Start lifting light and slowly increase the weight to reduce injuries. Consider using your own body weight in your exercise regimen if you've never used a weight.

If you haven't started a flexibility or stretching regimen it's time to implement this as part of your daily life. There are many different types of stretching and exercise regimens available that can work within your current physical limitations so don't be afraid to ask for help from a qualified professional. Don't be afraid to ask your trainer or physiotherapist what experience they have with working with someone with chronic pain or physical limitations. Remember, some movement is better than no movement. And if you are looking for something specific utilize Google and YouTube to uncover more as there are 1000s of resources available. Be specific in your search.

THE FASCIA – A MUCH-NEGLECTED AREA

One much neglected area when talking about mobility and healing is our fascial health. Fascia is the connective tissue that covers the muscles, nerves and blood vessels connecting every single cell in the body and it plays a key role in the body. It is essential for communicating information between cells and body systems and sending pain signals, affecting chronic inflammation and immune function. It helps the body with setting its circadian rhythm and much more. Dehydration, lack of movement and emotional trauma impede its ability to communicate and function properly.

Ensuring adequate water intake, working through the emotional effects of past trauma, dealing with emotional stress in healthy ways and improving mobility through movement, fascial release and stretching should be included as part of your healing journey. Stretching your hips and psoas muscles, which is an area which stores trauma, is beneficial for healing from trauma as trauma gets stuck in the fascia which can impede your healing journey (you can check out YouTube videos for how to release or stretch this area).

Fascia can become adhered and stuck, a common response to stress or the chronic tendency to suppress emotion. This is often known as guarding. When chronic stress and trauma get stuck in the fascia, the fascia becomes stiff and loses its fluidity causing tension and pain. This also inhibits the flow of information and contributes to a chronic holding or tension pattern in the tissues causing chronic pain, stiffness and restriction of movement. Surgery and scarring can also impede the fluid flow of information through the collagen and water that make up the grounding blocks of our fascia.

Massage and release of the fascia through gentle movement and stretching brings a rush of fresh hyaluronic acid and water to the area which can help release it. In doing so, traumatic memories that are stuck can be released and begin to integrate into your biology so that healing can begin.

We need supple bodies that can communicate effectively and fluidly within themselves, reacting appropriately to trauma and stress. When fascia is tended to, you are investing in overall health and wellness and are bringing a much-needed component to your healing journey. Fascial Stretch Therapy, Myofascial Release, Chinese Acupuncture and Physiotherapy are some options when consider additional support for fascial health, beyond general movement and stretching.

SUPPLEMENTS FOR MUSKULOSKELETAL PAIN, INFLAMMATION AND INJURY RECOVERY

Traumeel/Traumacare: One of my favourite homeopathic creams/ointments that is beneficial for reducing pain, bruising, inflammation from injury or sprains/strain, joint pain and muscle pain. It can speed healing for injury and inflammation to the musculoskeletal system. It can be used to reduce bruising as well.

Magnesium & Minerals: Magnesium is frequently depleted due to chronic stress. Magnesium comes in a variety of forms – but bisglycinate or glycinate can be helpful for relaxation. Potassium and sodium are needed for proper muscle function and to prevent cramping. See Tenet #4 to learn how to support healthy mineral balance.

DMSO (DIMETHYLSULFOXIDE): a wonderful topical compound for conditions such as bursitis, tendonitis and muscle pain to reduce pain and speed healing. It can be used externally on inflamed or sore muscles, tendons and ligaments. It has also been used for nerve pain but caution should be used when taking any medications.

As it enhances absorption of whatever other creams/lotions use caution when combining with other skin products. It can temporarily irritate the skin for some people causing itching or redness. There are books available on Amazon about DMSO use which might be helpful if you wish to learn more about this compound.

Tenet # 9: Tend to your Quantum Biological Terrain

I don't know about you, but when I started getting more interested in natural ways of healing, I would cringe at the word 'energy.' It just didn't seem very scientific when all I was familiar with was a biochemical approach to disease and healing. This biochemical approach meant that all acceptable medicines and treatments for disease had to be within this system. The biochemical approach is why 'acceptable' drugs are chemical compounds and treatments include cutting out diseased organs or tissues.

Health education rarely (if ever) discusses quantum biology or the body's energy or frequency (other than ATP and the cell) so I wasn't very open to anything that talked about energy as a therapy or treatment. However, as I uncovered, discovered and researched I came to a very overwhelming realization that we are energetic beings. Even our emotions have energy! I was shocked that there was research showing that we could measure the electromagnetic frequencies (EMF) of our body and that EMF had its own effects – positive and negative – on the body.

To give an amazing example of this: the heart puts off the largest electrical field of your whole body! Little wonder that a newborn is placed skin-to-skin with mom as a calming experience post birth.

Energy medicine is scientific, just not the type of science that most people are familiar with, given that most of us have grown up in societies where medicine has been reduced to a pure biochemical experience. We live in a world that easily rejects what it cannot yet explain or understand or can capitalize on. The system of healthcare we most frequently use treats the biochemical part of you and is geared towards performing procedures *on* you and *to* you because that can be somewhat externally controlled and influenced. However, the energetic part of our bodies are more within the personal domain and so, you can begin to support this powerful area.

It isn't far-fetched to consider that you need to begin tending to your body's energy given the incredible power of that energy on your health. You know now that emotions and trauma affect you physically. You are aware that EMF is a toxin that you are constantly exposed to living in this day and age. That all being said, you need to learn how to care for yourself using every available means.

For example, consider that emotions have energy that affects your health on every level. How can a doctor treat your emotions biochemically other than by altering the body in some drastic way through prescribing drugs or other external treatments? This approach doesn't deal with the root cause but is a Band-Aid and leaves the patient powerless. Only *you* can do the emotional work to bring your energy back into balance so that health can be restored. You are responsible for learning the skills and attending to your emotional needs.

Tending to your quantum terrain, the atomic makeup of your biology is a very deep, subtle, but incredibly powerful healing modality that should be regularly incorporated into our day-to-day life. <u>Don't underestimate the power of this healing modality just because it appears too simple or easy to perform.</u>

When you consider how exposed we are to unnatural energies in the form of Wi-Fi, 5G, our phones, computers, fluorescent lighting and how disconnected we are from nature's healing frequencies of natural light, soil, dirt, plants, fresh air, the sound of water, air and birds, it's unsurprising that so many of us are unwell. We need nature's healing energies to calm inflammation, set our circadian rhythm, boost mood and energy, balance our microbiome and more. These are foundational to health and get easily disrupted when we remain out of touch with nature.

I want to emphasize the ease of incorporating frequencies that heal into daily life. I want to impress upon you the fundamental need your body has for exposure to natural light, fresh air, regenerative soil and natural water. Consider the following recommendations as simple-but-powerful healing tools that should be daily incorporated into your lifestyle.

LIGHT

Morning sunlight: Direct morning sunlight exposure (without sunscreen or sunglasses) for 20 minutes before 10am increases your body's production of dopamine and serotonin which are essential for good mood. It helps set your circadian rhythm which is essential for hormone function and balance, good quality sleep and many other body functions.

Limit or stop using sunscreen and sunglasses: We do not need to protect ourselves from the sun or avoid sunlight. In fact, you can slowly build up your resistance to sunlight, preventing sunburn by increasing your exposure to sun over periods of days. Beginning in the springtime, get outside and expose yourself to the sun showing the most amount of skin possible. Daily, increase your time spent in the sun. This exposure helps your body adjust to the sun and tells your body to make more melanin, an antioxidant and the substance the protects your skin from UV light.

> Sunscreen use has been associated with an increase in skin cancer and is an endocrine disruptor. If there is no way to avoid direct sunlight for long periods, particularly during between the hours of 10am-4pm, you can consider using chemical-free sunscreen.
> Sunglasses also increase your risk of sunburn as your body is 'tricked' into thinking it is being exposed to less sunlight. As a result it doesn't make the needed amount of melanin to protect your skin increasing your risk of sunburn. I would recommend sunglasses when in direct sunlight for long periods of time or when on the water as it reflects light into the eyes. However, try using hats or staying in the shade instead of using sunglasses.
> Try using other sun protectants such as hats, staying in the shade and clothing containing SPF when you cannot avoid sunlight in the hottest parts of the day (10am-4pm).
> Eat a diet low in seed oils, high in various fruits and vegetables for their antioxidant potentional and supplementing Vitamin E also can help with UV radiation from sun exposure and can reduce your risk of burning.
> **_Use your own discretion as there are times or situations when sun protection has much needed benefits._**

Dimming lights at night: This helps with increasing the production of melatonin, your body's cancer scavenger, sleep aid and anti-inflammatory hormone. Dimming lights at night and avoiding blue light or screens can help you feel sleepier and is an important part of setting your circadian rhythm.

Get your Hands into Dirt/Soil: Getting your hands in the soil not only sends anti-inflammatory frequencies into your body promoting healing but it diversifies the gut microbiome bringing more robust health and boosting the immune system.

Humming, Singing, Gargling: These are all energetic and can stimulate your vagus nerve which plays a powerful role in your stress response. High vagal tone means increased resilience to chronic stress and trauma. Incorporating actions such as humming, singing, and gargling, into your daily life supports the vagus nerve which is responsible for communication between the gut, brain and the heart.

Sound therapy: Sound has energy that is emitted that can play a role in healing. Consider finding a YouTube or Spotify/Apple track of different sound frequencies that will help with whatever health concern you are dealing with. You can google Rife therapies for your specific issue and listen to that soundtrack. These soundtracks can help support mood, physical health issues and more.

Earthing/Grounding: Grounding is electrically conductive contact of the human body with the surface of the earth such as standing with shoes off in the sand, grass or swimming in the sea. Aim for 20 minutes a day. Earthrunners sell sandals that protect your feet while simultaneously grounding you. See Appendix A.

Get into nature: Swimming in oceans, rivers or lakes, walking in the forest and other activities that increase your exposure to natural elements will improve your quantum biology and positively affect your physical health.

Exercise: Enhance your quantum biology by increasing the production of nitric oxide which can improve cell function and communication. Aim for 30 minutes a day of exercise in the morning or early afternoon.

ADDITIONAL ENERGY HEALING THERAPIES

I'd like to introduce you to a few healing energy modalities that you can utilize at home or see a professional for treatment with. Homeopathic medicine, Chinese acupuncture, Pulsed Electromagnetic Frequency (PEMF) mats and grounding are some of my favourite healing modalities. These therapies can be used for so many health benefits including reducing inflammation, decreasing pain and muscle tension, supporting relaxation, reducing anxiety, helping with insomnia, speeding healing and more. As energy modalities they have a broad range of use for so many issues! Talking with a practitioner about your health issue and what might work is a helpful way to uncover a new healing therapy.

The following is not an exhaustive list of energetic modalities. Many are worth considering in your healing journey as they have profound ability and potential to bring about greater health. All of those listed below work on measurable scientific outcomes and theories.

- Homeopathic Medicine
- Chinese Acupuncture
- PEMF therapy – can be used for decreasing inflammation, speeding healing of injury, acute colds and flus, promoting

sleep, improving mood and concentration and much more. See Appendix A for purchasing a mat.
- ➢ Red Light Therapy – can be used to speed healing of deep tissues, reduce pain, and improve wound healing, to name a few things.
- ➢ RIFE therapy
- ➢ Sound therapy
- ➢ Hugs! ☺
- ➢ EFT (Emotional Freedom Technique) – uses tapping and vibration on the Chinese medicine meridians having a profound effect on our fascia.
- ➢ Myofascial release/massage
- ➢ Infrared sauna

Many practitioners utilizing energy therapies are not believers but the above listed therapies are scientific therapies so use your discernment when deciding if you wish to pursue treatment with them. Do not use that which feels uncomfortable for you as the point in using these is to bring healing and calm, not fear or distress. If the ideas of energy as healing is uncomfortable for you, pray through it and trust the Holy Spirit to give you wisdom as you make decision for your health that might be stretching and uncomfortable for you. God promises wisdom to those who ask Him – and this is true even for the area of health and wellness! He is the Great Physician and knows your body's needs.

Note: Reiki is considered an energy therapy that I would not recommend for Christians as practitioners of this channel energy from the 'universe' and go through a training where they receive special healing energy from a 'spirit.' This is a therapy that I would avoid.

Tenet #10: Slowing Down, Resting & Thankfulness

Last but not least, let's talk about the importance of slowing down, resting and enjoying the present. This is one area that I think the majority of us have a hard time making a regular part of our lifestyle. As soon as we feel better, we start to go, go, go, and then the body ends up in the same situation before: overstimulated, overwhelmed and having trouble healing. We have been told by society that productivity has value (if not the most value!) and we are so deeply entrenched in a system that pushes our productivity as a core marker of our worth that we are probably unaware of it. This is a large hurdle to healing!

Slowing down is *hard*. Even when I've seemingly stopped, I'm still 'busy' in my brain, planning this or that, or still running errands because I just enjoy being busy. There's no shame in that. I'm honestly not great at resting and I need to rest to care well for myself. I still revert to old patterns of pushing through stress, delay dealing with my emotions, over-rationalizing my feelings and physically pushing myself as soon as my symptoms have settled. I stop the journalling as soon as I'm 'better' and am surprised that 5 weeks later I'm emotionally at my end and I have a new flare up. This might be your pattern as well.

We often forget to enjoy the present and engage fully with the moment. We can easily attempt to ignore our body's signals of distress until it's too late. When we get to this point, do not despair; sometimes our greatest growth happens *because* of the pain. When we choose to engage with it, rather than ignore it or minimize or move away from it there are untold stories of incredible growth and healing because it can free us to move on. This may be easier to do when you remember that God is present with you in every moment. He is the true rest and entering into that rest with Him and abiding in Him is restorative on levels that we cannot fully comprehend.

Healing doesn't happen overnight and when your symptoms are from a lifetime of poor choices and habits, you will definitely need to invest in a complete lifestyle overhaul where rest is a foundation to your wellness. You need to learn to create a new way of being that incorporates and practices rests as a regular, daily, part of your life. There was a very real purpose for God's institution of Sabbath rest. Yes, you do need to work but you are also required to rest and care for your body as it is a temple of the Holy Spirit. To do this, you may need to change the way you live life for both the present and the future regardless of your current health status.

Begin by taking the pressure off yourself and being compassionate with yourself! When you slow right down and stop comparing yourself to how you felt years ago and expecting that old you to reappear you are doing yourself a service. You are where you are now and that is your starting point.

Adopt an attitude of thankfulness for where you are today, the challenges you have overcome and all that you have learned in your healing journey. It's in the slowness, the rest and the practicing of self-compassion that you will find more peace and a body more receptive and able to heal.

God has brought me on a long journey of health. I still fight day to day to remain as symptom free as possible. But I am not the me of 15 years ago. I have struggled and overcome disappointment. I have become more resilient and have a greater sense of my value. I have developed emotional skills and worked through some hard emotional pains. I have learned to pray and wrestle with God for many things. I am learning to slow down and truly see the gift of the discipline of rest as a fundamental part of the Christian life. I am learning to embrace each moment, the ups and downs, engaging with my feelings of grief and disappointment and inviting Jesus into that process.

I am beginning to understand the gift that *now* has and realize that the absence of pain or struggle is sadly not going to happen this side of heaven even when I am fully well because we live in a broken world. There will always be something that is difficult or hard, whether it's my own or someone else I love has to wrestle through it. We need joy that is not dependent on our circumstances.

Lastly, I would encourage you to regularly schedule in time to rest – either a rest where you are creative, when you move your body or where you can engage with your deepest heart needs. Create time to do nothing and just be. Spend time with your Creator and drink from His refreshing Presence. Cultivate an attitude of thankfulness as this can shift your mind and emotions which will influence your health. Pour out your heart to Him unapologetically. Your deepest place of belonging is where He is…and He is always with you because, as His Child He is in you. You don't need to strive or prove or do. Enjoy being fully loved for who you are and not what you've done.

Part 6

Finding Wholeness: Our Spiritual Life as a Foundation to Health

Though outwardly we are wasting away, yet inwardly we are being renewed day by day.
– 2 Cor. 4:16

And so we reach the last and final section of this book. The work, time, energy and reflection that you have invested up till this point have been a vital and foundational part of your healing journey. To make this a truly holistic journey there is one more sphere that I want to explore with you because it is an essential piece of the healing picture: the spiritual sphere. I want to walk you through some questions and thoughts around your spiritual life and its connection to your physical, mental and emotional health.

It is in the spiritual part of your being wherein you will find the freedom and healing you desperately need in the midst of living with whatever health limitations or struggles you experience this side of heaven. I know that not everyone working through this book will hold to the same spiritual perspectives and beliefs as I do and that's okay. But I want to be clear that I wrote this section with the understanding and belief that ultimately the greatest healing we can ever receive this side of heaven is a restored relationship with our Creator God through Jesus Christ.

God is living and actively involved in your life and He wants to be in an intimate, personal relationship with you. He desperately loves you, wants to speak with you, help you and heal you. I would encourage you to spend time with Him in prayer and read your Bible as you go through this section, expecting Him to show up to minister to your soul and spirit. No matter what your personal circumstances are today, when you live in a restored relationship with your Creator, you carry the delightful promise and hope that you will one day be fully reunited with Jesus in heaven. There He will wipe away every tear and heal every disease. That is a powerful encouragement and hope!

Prayerfully approach the questions and answers in this chapter and ask God for wisdom and understanding as God is the ultimate authority on all things health and healing. The Holy Spirit is your Counsellor and your Guide and He promises to reveal truth. He shines light into areas of darkness and confusion. He will bring you clarity, understanding and peace if you ask for it.

I have written this section differently than the previous chapters. Instead of asking questions and having you answer them on your own, I have shared some of the most popular and pertinent questions I have asked around the connection between health and healing and our spiritual life. Some of these questions came about as I worked with patients in my practice, attempting to understand why healing didn't occur at times. Others came out of my personal health struggles and experiences. I have then answered them for you.

You will see that the questions have already been answered. These answers are meant to encourage thoughts but are not meant to tell you what to believe. There may be ideas that sound controversial to you. I will say that what I have written comes from my personal experience and healing journey, books that I have read, thoughts that I have wrestled through and the result of much prayer, discernment and time spent reading God's Word.

Some of the following questions might be triggering for you, some will bounce right off and some will induce deeper thought. Not everything written will be relatable or relevant to you or your situation. May the questions and answers stimulate greater thought, draw you into His word and most importantly, bring you into greater intimacy and deeper relationship with the One who loves you and heals you.

Why does sickness occur?

The bible teaches us that God is the Creator of all and He deeply loves His creation which includes you! He created you in His image and His desire is intimate relationship with you. Sin and brokenness entered the world when Adam and Eve disobeyed God (you can read how this occurred in the Bible in Genesis 2-3) and their perfect relationship with the Creator God was severed. This broken relationship meant that every human being born into this world would experience the consequence of broken relationship in the form of both spiritual and physical death. This spiritual and physical death meant that we could no longer live in a loving relationship with God for eternity. Instead, our sinfulness separated us from our Holy Creator, dooming us to live in sin, experiencing disease, death and brokenness in our physical bodies. Spiritual death meant that we became blind and deaf to the One who created us, unable to hear clearly from God, restricting access to lifegiving, loving relationship with Him, leaving us confused and frustrated as to our identity and purpose. However, God had a plan of hope for humanity in the midst of this!

God knows all things, the end from the beginning. God's intention when He created the world was never and has never been for us to be sick. Yet, that is what happened as a result of sin –especially as we age and experience pain and trauma from living in a world filled with broken and hurting people. Do not give up hope though! God loves us deeply and so He made a way through His Son Jesus for us to be returned into a loving relationship with Him, making us spiritually alive once again. You can be restored into relationship with God through Christ when you confess that Jesus is your Lord and Saviour, when you repent of your sin and then live a life of obedience to Him and His Word. When Jesus returns again those who have been restored to Jesus will then fully experience physical renewal and healing and complete spiritual perfection.

Does my level of faith affect whether God will heal me?

This was a question I struggled with many times in my own personal health journey. Loving Christians would pray for me and declare healing over my body and then ask me to do something that might prove the immediate efficacy of the prayer. Had my pain disappeared? Could I now walk without pain? Often, the answer was no. Then they would pray again believing that God would instantly heal. Again, I would still be left with pain and symptoms. I would leave that prayer session feeling like *I* was a failure. I felt that *my* faith was somehow lacking and that I was somehow responsible for not being healed.

There were times I would feel guilty or question if I had enough faith that God could heal. Maybe it was my level of faith that was the reason why I wasn't receiving healing then and there. I would even get angry with these good-intentioned believers because they had no idea that the lack of healing made me question or doubt my faith.

I believe that many Christians struggling with health issues have at some point felt similarly to how I felt and have experiences similar to what I described. They have questioned their faith and they have wrestled with guilt or shame when they don't see the results that others or they themselves expect to see when prayers of healing are offered in faith. Be encouraged! God is a lot more powerful and loving and wise than you can imagine! There is much more to be explored when it comes to faith and healing.

Over the years I have arrived at several conclusions around faith and healing. Faith is necessary for healing, yes, but God can heal in spite of our lack of faith. For someone to receive healing there must be faith – but that burden doesn't fall only on the person with the sickness. In fact, the person praying in faith is enough for healing to occur! In Matthew 9:2 it says, "Some men brought to him [Jesus] a paralyzed man, lying on a mat. When Jesus saw *their* [italics mine] faith, he said to the man, "Take heart, son; your sins are forgiven." That man was healed and he picked up his mat and walked away. The text says nothing about the man's faith. Rather, it clearly says that his friends had faith for him to be healed. Clearly, that was enough!

We know that Jesus' ability to perform miracles where there was no faith was limited but it wasn't impossible (Matt. 15:38).

This is very encouraging! God is greater than our level of faith and can move in spite of our lack of faith. Remember that faith as small as a mustard seed can move a mountain; so even the tiniest bit of faith can be enough for healing. So, no, you don't need a lot of faith (or even any at times) to be healed. In fact, when you consider the healing that can occur when an unbeliever receives healing from a prayer offered by a Christian praying in, it shows that faith on the part of the sick person isn't always required. Ultimately, when healing occurs from a prayer offered in faith, someone has faith for healing, either the person doing the praying or the person receiving the healing prayer, but both are not necessary.

With that being said, a pray offered in faith does not guarantee immediate healing either. This has to do with God's design, timing and will being accomplished, something we as humans don't fully understand or see. Timing in God's kingdom is important. God's timing in your healing journey is very important. God deeply cares about you and your health. He knows the how, the when, the where and the why to your healing. So, when you don't see healing now, even if you have faith, it doesn't mean that God isn't working on it or won't do it at a later date. We don't know God's thoughts or intentions or timing but you can trust that they are good even if you don't feel that in your current situation.

When you don't see healing you can rest in God's divine loving care for every aspect of your health and your life. Share your frustrations, discouragement, lack of faith around healing and anger over your health with Him. He tells us in Psalm 62:8, "Trust in him at all times, you people; pour out your hearts to him, for God is our refuge." He knows your heart and He wants you to share it with Him. Your honesty is not a sign of lack of faith but evidence of real, intimate relationship with Him and speaks of a surrender and trust that He is still God over your health.

Do not despair while you wait for healing. He carries you, holds you, remains faithful when you are faithless and His willingness or ability to heal is not impeded by or dependent on your level of faith in His ability to heal you. He is the Great Physician and He is your Faithful Father. Faithful He is and Faithful He will continue to be wherever you are on your healing journey.

Does God still heal today?

I am a living testimony of God's ability to heal today! So, yes!! God heals today and continues to heal. My experience has been that He can heal immediately, over time (years even!), through prayer, by the laying on of hands, through doctors and natural health professionals, through medicines and natural herbs and in a myriad of other ways. In the Bible, Jesus was always healing in different ways – in fact, he never healed someone in the same way twice!

Some Christians believe that God doesn't heal or very rarely heals today, but I strongly disagree – not only because I have seen it, experienced it and have heard many testimonies of God doing supernatural healing, but also because God does not change. He healed in the past and He can and does heal now. His desire *is* for healing – not just the physical, but the emotional, mental and spiritual parts of you. Every part of who you are matters to Him. What this means for you is that God is interested in making you whole, completely restored and healthy in every area of your being.

Spiritual healing entails being restored into relationship with Him. That is the most important piece to true healing, because when you are restored back into relationship with God, it helps you to live out your identity as His child. The intimacy of that relationship and His clearly defined purpose for your life and identity feeds into that abundant life He promises His children (John 10:10). Not only that, but you live with hope of full physical, mental and emotional healing in heaven. God can heal physical disease in spite of a lack of relationship with Him, however, when we are in restored relationship with Him, we experience the greatest benefits now and into eternity.

Although God can and does heal today, there is no guarantee that you will experience partial or full healing while you are on earth. God's desire may be to physically heal you, but it may not be His timing or His will for you at present. His timing and His ways are not ours and we often can't understand or comprehend those ways or plans. This can be disappointing and frustrating at times. However, you can rest in the knowledge that right now He sees you and loves you and that He has the full picture that you may not see. God works through every circumstance for the good of those who love him (Rom. 8:28). Don't give up on praying for healing! Just because the answer may be 'not now' does not mean that it is 'not ever.'

Is sin at the root of my symptoms or illness?

In John 9:2-12 Jesus addresses the disciples' question of sin being the cause of blindness in a young man born blind. They wondered whether sin on the part of the young man or his parents was at the root of his condition. Jesus responds saying, "It was not that this man sinned, or his parents, but that the works of God might be displayed in him." This story shows that although sin can play a role in sickness it is not necessarily right to assume so. Rather, God can and does use our health struggles to bring glory to Himself.

To further discuss how sin can play a role in sickness we need to look at how sin affects us as human beings. Sinful behaviours and sinful thoughts, particularly on-going and repetitive sin, can be opportunities for the devil to attack you. Disobedience and thoughts that are not in line with God's Word can become footholds for Satan to influence us and weaken us. These areas of disobedience become areas of vulnerability. Satan will use our weaknesses and vulnerabilities to further weaken us and draw us away from relationship with God.

Our minds and our thought lives, particularly as they pertain to our identity and our beliefs about God, are frequent areas of target by Satan. At the end of the day, these unsubmitted areas of thought and action leaves us susceptible to attack and can result in sickness of the body, mind and spirit. Consider how our thoughts and our beliefs around our identity have influence over our health as discussed in previous sections of this book.

Psalm 32: 1-5 addresses some physical effects of living in sin.
"Blessed is the one
    whose transgressions are forgiven,
    whose sins are covered.
Blessed is the one
    whose sin the Lord does not count against them
    and in whose spirit is no deceit.

When I kept silent,
    my bones wasted away
    through my groaning all day long.
For day and night
    your hand was heavy on me;
my strength was sapped
    as in the heat of summer.

Then I acknowledged my sin to you
    and did not cover up my iniquity.
I said, "I will confess

> my transgressions to the Lord."
> And you forgave
> the guilt of my sin."

Why physical health can be negatively affected by sinful beliefs or behaviours is not something I fully understand, but it is clear from this text that your body, mind and spirit can suffer sickness if there is unrepentant sin. You will reap bad fruit if you are sowing bad seeds.

God wants our whole hearts. He wants our minds and our thought lives, our emotions, and our entire obedience to Him in every aspect. Continued daily surrender, obedience to His Word and repentance forms the foundation to our Christian lives. Don't let shame or fear hold you captive to on-going or habitual sin. Don't continue feeding lies about your identity, your value and worth, or about how past traumas or experiences have made you into a 'lesser-than' person.

Areas of known sin where there is unrepentance and on-going disobedience need to be dealt with. Don't give the devil any foothold in your life as he will exploit any and every weakness. Healing can occur in every part of your being, and as you work through every area of healing, God can and will set you free! When you surrender every part of yourself to Jesus and speak His truth over yourself and repent of sinful beliefs or disobedience, you create opportunity for the Spirit to heal, redeem and restore.

If you truly are convicted that your sickness is stemming from sin in your life and want to be set free then it is time to repent. I would highly recommend connecting with a Pastor or trusted fellow Christian to confess your sin, get wisdom and insight into this area in your life, pray through this and ultimately repent of whatever it is that is at the root of your illness. Wise counsel is highly advised, as is personal accountability so that you do not return to a lifestyle of sin. Although this does not guarantee that physical healing will occur instantaneously, it will bring health to your soul and spirit which will feed into your physical, mental and emotional health.

Are demonic influences causing my sickness?

This is a hard question to answer, not because there isn't an answer to this question, but more so because I think many Christians have not given much thought to the spiritual realm of darkness. We are often uncomfortable with discussions on this topic or we simply lack knowledge when it comes to this subject. As believers we know that we are in a spiritual battle and it rages around us. We are told that the devil prowls around like a roaring lion looking for someone to devour (1 Peter 5:8). He desires us to be sick and unhealed because he comes to steal, kill and destroy (John 10:10).

> NOTE: When I am talking about demonic attack this is not the same thing as demon possession. Believers cannot be possessed as they owned by God, are Spirit-filled and we can only belong to one master. However, believers can be attacked by the enemy and his agents.

Demonic influence on health is a very real thing and it does occur in today's world. It is something we need to be aware of in our healing journey because it can play a part in the physical, mental or emotional symptoms we experience. Discerning if your health issues are from demonic attack requires prayer and discernment and godly, wise and discerning counsel. Although I want to point out that we shouldn't be quick to say that demonic attack is the sole reason for your symptoms or health, neither should we be too quick to dismiss that it may play a role in the symptoms you experience.

We are told that as believers we are more than conquerors through Him who loves us (Rom. 8:37) and that we have been given divine power to demolish spiritual strongholds (2 Cor. 10:4). As such, we are not without weapons of warfare when it comes to the spiritual battles we face (Ephesians 6). However, I think there is a general disbelief or ignorance that demons could have any influence in our lives as believers. We somehow fall into thinking that God would never allow demons to attack us.

Demons are very real and they do attack believers. They are agents of Satan who want to kill, steal and destroy us and to draw us away from a loving and life-giving relationship with God. Satan will use whatever means necessary to exploit our vulnerabilities and weaken our relationship with God.

Some believers may argue that the blood of Jesus protects us from demonic attack. Jesus, in His grace, does protect us from things that we are often not aware of. However, as believers we are also told to *exert* our spiritual authority and *use* the weapons of our warfare. This means that we are also to be actively *engaged* in warfare. Although we are covered with Jesus' blood and He does protect us from more than we can possibly imagine, we are susceptible to demonic influence and attack. This is due to the brokenness of the world we live in, our own humanity and sinfulness and the fact that we are in the midst of an ongoing spiritual battle.

Satan is deceptive and cunning. He knows our areas of weakness and will do whatever he can to exploit those areas. We aren't always on guard, we *do* choose to believe lies about God and ourselves, we hide shame and brokenness and hurt and we do experience trauma from others. These are areas of vulnerability and they are areas where we can experience spiritual attack. These attacks can appear in the form of physical, emotional and mental health issues.

Trauma makes us vulnerable in every way imaginable and can be viewed as an assault on our very person, violating personal, spiritual, physical and emotional boundaries. This violation can be used by the devil as a foothold (or entrance point) for attacks on the mental, physical, spiritual or emotional areas of your life. These attacks can appear in various forms including negative thoughts, thoughts of self-harm and self-hatred, mental or emotional disorders such as hearing voices, mood swings and more. The devil really likes to attack your mind because this is a powerful area. Our mind influences every aspect of our being including our beliefs, our emotions, our decisions and our actions.

The development of health issues or mental/emotional disorders after trauma does not mean that it is of demonic origin. In fact, your health issues could be from the emotional impact of the trauma and not dealing with the emotions in healthy ways afterwards. This needs to be said and is a reminder that the emotional impact of trauma needs to be worked through in your healing journey. However, I would like to further explore how experiencing trauma and/or living with unrepentant sin or areas of disobedience make us susceptible to demonic attack in our health.

Trauma creates footholds for the enemy to attack because the violation or wounds caused by these experiences often generate questions and lies around God's character and goodness. It is also not uncommon after traumatic experiences that we take on heavy burdens of shame, guilt, fear, failure, self-hatred, rage or anger or lies around our identity. The violation of personal boundaries, the shock of an experience we were unprepared for and the weakness of our humanity can contribute to the emotional and spiritual pain. Trauma and the weight of shame afterwards lead many to hide what happened and the secrecy allows more shame and destruction to take root which the enemy prays on. Darkness is a place where the enemy thrives and feeds.

Coping strategies after traumatic experiences may include sinful behaviours such as self-harm, addictive behaviours, sexual sin or drug use, and although they may temporarily bring false relief, they ultimately bring about destruction and feed into the shame. Although the above-mentioned responses to trauma are often considered normal human responses, they are harmful and can also be used (or caused!) by demonic influence to continue to feed into shame and attack our identity, our health and our spiritual life.

To be clear, I am not saying that demonic attack in your life is your fault. This is not a matter of fault and this discussion is not about laying blame or bringing shame. We are vulnerable human beings in a broken world, we are and always will be under spiritual attack and our humanity and weakness make us vulnerable. Satan exploits this weakness and vulnerability. He wants you feeling ashamed and to hide away. He wants you to feel that you are powerless. This is even easier to do when you are physically or mentally run down or discouraged. This is why God has given us weapons of warfare and spiritual authority as His sons and daughters. He hasn't left us powerless.

I wanted to share with you my own experience with demonic attack and the effects it had on my health. In 2017 I began to develop severe insomnia along with thoughts of self-harm and self-hatred. This occurred during a period of my life where I was dealing with a lot of personal, professional and physical/emotional health issues. The onset of the thoughts of self-harm and self-hatred came after a painful interaction with a health professional I was in the care of. This health provider verbally attacked my relationship with Jesus and my identity as a child of God. He then proceeded to violate some physical boundaries.

The shock of an attack by a person who was supposed to be safe made me vulnerable emotionally and spiritually. The violation of the physical boundaries made me feel ashamed and as a result I didn't fully share with anyone what had happened because I felt that somehow, I was responsible for what had happened. What was happening in my life was in one sense, the perfect storm. My shame around those events led me to keep the event hidden, creating an opportunity that the devil took full advantage of. Keeping things hidden allowed for more shame and for lies around my identity to fester.

The onset of the insomnia was severe and was accompanied by intense thoughts of self-hatred and self-harm. These were thoughts that I had never experienced in my life before. The next months were extremely difficult as I continued to experience nightly spiritual attacks; I felt such hatred towards myself which fed into a desire to hurt myself. These horrible thoughts were often forgotten during the day as I was busy with work, but the lack of sleep led to major emotional instability making me further ashamed. I felt that I was living in a nightmare that I couldn't seem to escape.

It was almost two years later that God revealed to me that the lies I was believing about my identity, that the shame I was carrying and the thoughts of self-harm were connected to all the life events I had been dealing with, but particularly to the health visit I had been through years previously. I felt deeply convicted that the attacks and thoughts of hate and self-harm were playing a big part in my sleeplessness. He didn't leave me there though…He showed me how to break free because that is what He does!

Prayer, transparency and repentance were fundamental in breaking up this ongoing, nightly spiritual attack. The first step was exposing shame and allowing the hidden to come to light. I felt deeply convicted of a need to repent for the lie surrounding my value and worth and of speaking those words of hatred over myself at night. I repented of doubting my identity in Christ. I broke agreement with the lies I had believed about myself and I claimed the Father's words of love for me as His child. I declared freedom over myself.

When I repented of those lies and prayed God's protection over myself, the voices of self-harm and self-hatred left and never came back. Since that night all those years ago I have not felt anxiety as intense as that, I have not felt the need to hurt myself or tell myself that I hate myself and my insomnia started healing that very day after years of suffering. Praise Jesus!

I share my experience with you to show how physical health can be influenced by the thoughts you think and the experiences or traumas that occur in your life. For myself, there was sin that I felt convicted of and needed to repent of. That was crucial in my healing journey. My identity had always been an area I struggled with and that traumatic experience was exploited by Satan to weaken me further. Repentance and aligning myself with God's truth began the physical healing of my insomnia. But even more so, it created greater spiritual freedom and a deeper walk of intimacy with Jesus.

God's healing hand is always held out towards us. There is no sin or trauma too great that His blood and love cannot cover it. God does and can bring healing from sin and trauma from years ago. What an incredible Saviour He is! There is no demon that He cannot overcome. That is the power of the cross. Satan is a defeated enemy and do not forget that!

As you wrestle through the question, "Are demonic influences causing my sickness?" I would encourage you to pray and ask God to expose any areas of your life where you are allowing sin or false beliefs to dictate your life or the way you think. Sin and false beliefs are areas for surrender and repentance with the wonderful goal of life-giving freedom in Christ! If you started to develop physical health issues or mental or emotional symptoms or addictive behaviours after trauma you can pray for and declare freedom over yourself using the Spirit-filled authority you have as a son or daughter of the Most High God. You can receive healing.

You may need to walk through the trauma with a counsellor and work through the emotions that have been left unexplored or unprocessed. If, after doing that work, you still are experiencing these issues, there may be a spiritual component at play. Obviously, I am not saying that if you have done all the emotional work and spiritual freedom work that your symptoms will automatically disappear. That can be the outcome, but it can also be a process that occurs over time.

Lastly, I want to encourage you: do not let this discussion create any kind of fear in you. Praise God that we do not need to fear a defeated enemy, his demons or those who oppose us. Fear is from the enemy and it makes us vulnerable. You have not been given a spirit of fear, but of power, love and soundness of mind (2 Tim. 1:7). You do not have to fear because He is *your* Defender and He is committed to defending you and setting you free. You are more than a conqueror through Christ and you overcome by His blood and the word of your testimony (Rev. 12:11)! Just think! Your testimony of His work in your life – His healing power and the freedom He is working out in your life – is a weapon! Greater is He who is in you then he [Satan] who is in the world (1 John 4:4).

Let those truths serve as your daily reminder that you are protected and you can pick up your weapons of warfare. You are not powerless. If you need to repent of sin or lies – repent! If you feel the need to command the enemy to leave in a specific way – command him to leave in the name of Jesus! Jesus' name is the ultimate Authority and it is powerful over every spiritual being and all things. Pray the blood of Jesus over the areas where you have been set free and seal them in His name.

Using wisdom and discernment in our life and healing journey is essential. If there is concern about demonic influence in your life there are many godly pastors and ministries that can help you discern through this and help set you free. Pray for direction and wisdom in who to invite into this journey because He will faithfully provide it.

> A word of caution as you deal with this – God is gracious with us but if you are not truly interested in being free of lies or sin it is best to pray and ask God to change your heart so that true repentance occurs. You want total freedom and complete healing. Don't exchange half-truths for lies or somewhat free for full freedom.

Can I expect healing?

God's intention and design before the fall into sin in the Garden of Eden was health and wholeness for every human. So, yes, you can expect that healing will occur, because His desire for human beings to be whole and healthy has not and will not change. However, whether you will experience healing this side of heaven is not a promise. Why? Because while in this world we are still subject to the brokenness of this world. That being said, His design for you is wholeness and to fully restore you. What this means for you is that His first and greatest desire is a healed relationship with Him. This is so you can enjoy the benefit of His loving Presence now, be fully healed in heaven and then spend an eternity with Him. That is what I am referring to when I speak of His promise and design to make you whole.

> *His desire for human beings to be whole and healthy
> has not and will not change.*

You can ask God for healing, declare it prophetically over yourself and believe for it because God truly desires His children be healed and whole. It is also important to remember that God's purpose for you now is to make you more like Christ and to build His kingdom. This means that if your sickness and physical struggles are being used in some inexplicable way to draw you closer to Himself, make you more like Christ and build His Kingdom, your healing may occur, it may partially occur or it may not happen at all while here on earth. Whatever serves His Kingdom first and brings the most glory to His name.

Although, this may not seem fair, I want to remind you (as I often remind myself), that our lives must be all about Him and for Him: *all* of my life, my health and my being. He promises good and perfect gifts to His children. He is constantly loving you in ways that don't always seem clear with our earthly and limited understanding and perspectives. We were not told that we would have an easy life or a life without struggle or pain. We are told that He will work in everything for our good (Rom 8:28) and that He will be your strength when you are weak.

Accepting these truths can be a daily, if not minute-by-minute struggle, full of emotional and spiritual ups and downs. However, He promises to be with you, using your weaknesses and sickness to bring Him glory whilst giving you strength to persevere. He promises that He will make you more like Christ and that you can expect healing in all its fullness when you step into heaven with Him (Rev. 21:4).

What does it mean to experience healing?

This question connects to the earlier question "Does God still heal today?" but it goes a bit deeper than that. Yes, you can definitely experience healing this side of heaven. In my personal experience with my health, I would say healing takes place over time, is often slow, is emotionally and spiritually charged, but it can occur. However, *God is interested in healing every part of you.* We often are more interested in getting rid of specific symptoms or health issues. We have a definition of what we think healing is (and it often is that to some extent!) and we push for it, often ignoring areas of our lives where we are living in bondage to things such as our painful past, emotional or spiritual wounds, anxiety, fear, anger, addiction and more.

We often are more interested in getting rid of specific symptoms or health issues, often ignoring areas of our lives where we are living in bondage to things such as our painful past, emotional or spiritual wounds, anxiety, fear, anger, addiction and more. **God is interested in healing every part of you.**

His desire for you is to live an abundant, joy-filled, peace-rich and free life now. How does that sound to you? I want the healing that brings *that* type of life into existence and makes me able to enjoy that every day. When we experience healing in every sphere of our lives (mentally, physically, emotionally, spiritually) we become who God created us to be, our potential is unlocked and we walk with the greatest authority, the deepest of relationship with Him and with true purpose and clarity. It is in finding out and living out our identity and calling in His service that we experience true freedom and soul-deep healing. To be truly free and living out a life like that is one of my greatest desires.

As God heals every part of your person – the mental, emotional, spiritual and physical – He takes you, gently and patiently, through a process. This holistic and loving approach brings healing to the emotional pains of your past. It invites and equips you to walk in deeper intimacy with Him. It develops your authority in areas unique to your struggles and calling and through this process He reveals your unique identity.

If that is the deep and holistic healing that God knows you need, because He formed and created you, then, yes, you can and will experience healing. *It is a holistic, root-cause, every sphere, all-in approach.* He knows you best, He knows your potential, the best timing and the best way. For some it might mean living with some physical, mental or emotional symptoms but walking in greater peace, joy and closer intimacy and dependency on your Heavenly Father.

When we experience healing in every sphere of our lives (mentally, physically, emotionally, spiritually) we become who God created us to be, our potential is unlocked and we walk with the greatest authority, the deepest of relationship with Him and with true purpose and clarity. It is in finding out and living out our identity and calling in His service that we experience true freedom and soul-deep healing.

I am not fully physically healed as I write this book. But I can say that the healing God has brought to my heart at this point in my story – teaching me how to rest, to trust His love, goodness and timing for my life, revealing deeper parts of Himself, holding and carrying me when I am at my weakest, greater emotional health, helping me to understand my ability and potential and teaching me to walk in my identity with boldness and authority and even writing this book! – has brought greater peace with the physical symptoms and daily struggles I experience. I am learning more and more how to let go of my own agenda and truly, utterly rest in Him, His goodness and His timing. That to me has been my greatest healing.

Does it mean I don't wrestle with my health, disappointment and emotional discouragements at times? Not at all! I am still a human and my desire is to be fully pain and symptom free. However, I can trust that my physical weakness enables God's power to be shown all the more in me (2 Cor. 12:19). I may not like my lot in life at times but I can trust that He is good to me and committed to making me more like Christ. It's His way and His timing.

When reading scripture accounts of Jesus healing people, we often see how he addresses the physical and the spiritual interchangeably. For example, in Matthew 9:5-6 Jesus says, "Which is easier: to say, 'Your sins are forgiven,' or to say, 'Get up and walk?' But so that you may know that the Son of Man has authority on earth to forgive sins..." Then He said to the paralytic, "Get up, pick up your mat, and go home." I was confused by this until I felt the Holy Spirit give me this *aha!* moment of understanding.

Jesus can and does heal physically but His greatest desire for you is spiritual healing. **He knows that there can be no eternal wholeness or long-term physical healing without the healing of the soul that comes in the form of a restored relationship with Him.** To be clear, this verse does not say that Jesus only heals physically *if* or *when* there is spiritual healing. He wants *both* for you. This is why, as you pursue your physical, mental or emotional healing, you need tools that will give you a holistic perspective on your health. You need to be equipped for healing that is deep and truly lifegiving!

When Jesus heals, his true interest is in whole person healing – the spiritual, mental, emotional and physical.

What does it mean to prophetically declare healing over myself?

A prophetic declaration of healing is an act of faith where you stand aligned with the truth that God's design for you is health, healing and wholeness. It's a statement that you believe He is able to heal, He can heal you and that you know that Jesus' death paid for your healing. It is a declaration of trust that God's timing is good, that He hears your desires and that He is committed to your healing.

Psalm 103:1-5 is a wonderful prayer that is also a declaration. Pray it over yourself! Declare the words of His Word over your body and your health.

"Praise the Lord, my soul;
  all my inmost being, praise his holy name.
Praise the Lord, my soul,
  and forget not all his benefits—
who forgives all your sins
  and heals all your diseases,
who redeems your life from the pit
  and crowns you with love and compassion,
who satisfies your desires with good things

so that your youth is renewed like the eagle's."

Can I experience a full life with joy and freedom when I still struggle with my health?

I think the answer to anyone reading this is an obvious and resounding yes! However, actually living that out amongst daily physical, mental and emotional struggles is a lot harder. I still live with physical health challenges and, yes, I have experienced physical healing. But I am still pursuing more healing. I hope that you feel that is true for you as well! However, I want you to walk away from this workbook with a deep sense of peace, joy and freedom even whilst you struggle with health issues, mental, emotional or physical.

How do you do this? I know that the most obvious and effective way to live and know this experience of peace and joy is with daily reminders of Biblical truths that speak to the hurting areas of your heart. The Word of God is living, active and it pierces deep within. It brings life, correction if needed, hope and peace. It contains promises that we can claim as God's children.

Secondly, I believe one of the deepest ways to experience abundant life in the midst of struggle is through abiding in Jesus. This can happen through speaking truth over yourself and spending time with Him in prayer, reading His word, singing worship and sitting in silence with Him. In His presence is fullness of joy (Psalm 16:11).

When I abide in the truth of His word and encounter Jesus, I more easily am able to come to a place of rest and surrender amidst my circumstances. He in turn fills me with His Presence of Peace, Truth, Hope and Life. There are days when the words of Scripture don't always 'feel' true in the moment, but with continued reminders, claiming the truths as mine and spending time with Him, I do find more joy and peace. Examples of the truths that I speak to myself or meditate on include Bible verses or simple phrases such as: He loves me, He is with me, He is for me, He provides for me, He fights for me, His timing is perfect, He is my healer, He gives me peace, He holds me, and He is with me.

Thirdly, I claim joy and peace as mine through His Holy Spirit even if I don't feel it. Both joy and peace are ours even when we don't feel them or believe them. They are a fruit of His Spirit living within us and His promise to us as His children. I cannot always change my circumstances or my health but I can claim this joy and peace by surrendering myself and my life to Him. I can pursue His Kingdom first even with a failing body (Matt 5:24). I can find peace and joy in the knowledge that when I seek Him first, He will provide for all my needs in any given moment even as I deal with health struggles. James 1:2-4 speaks of trials building perseverance, growing us into maturity and complete children of God.

Not only that, I know that I am building up treasure for an eternal Kingdom which won't be destroyed and where I one day will find myself fully healed. My health struggles aren't the sum value of my life and do not dictate or define my life's purpose. Yes, He can and does use those struggles to build His Kingdom when I commit my way to His direction and will. This is so encouraging because I know God will bring beauty from ashes and He is in the business or restoration. I ask for Him to give me peace and joy no matter the circumstances I find myself in and that He would be glorified in whatever I accomplish, but most importantly, through who I am. I love the reminder in 2 Cor. 4: 7-12 of how our we are jars of clay with external weakness but living out eternal life,

> "But we have this treasure in jars of clay to show that this all-surpassing power is from God and not from us. We are hard pressed on every side, but not crushed;

perplexed, but not in despair; persecuted, but not abandoned; struck down, but not destroyed. We always carry around in our body the death of Jesus, so that the life of Jesus may also be revealed in our body. For we who are alive are always being given over to death for Jesus' sake, so that his life may also be revealed in our mortal body. So then, death is at work in us, but life is at work in you."

Fourthly, I prophetically declare healing over myself and call forth His promised abundant life as mine. What this means is calling forth of His desire for wholeness in me and a declaration that it is happening even if I don't see it in this moment. God then, through prayer and in relationship with Him, repositions my heart to accept whatever physical situation I find myself in that day. It is not a defeatist acceptance that I will be 'sick forever,' but a belief that He gives me what I need to thrive today, He has a future planned for me and He is delighted with me today no matter how I see myself or what I am able to accomplish.

In conclusion

I started this book with a chapter on identity because it is an essential foundation to your healing. I end with a chapter on freedom and wholeness and its relation to our spiritual health because it vital to your thriving as a human in the midst of a broken world. It is essential for your wellness in the midst of struggle and pain. You can find hope when you know you have a loving heavenly Father and a faithful Friend on the journey. It is in your deepest surrender, including being honest and open with your desires and disappointment, and the laying down of your pain at His feet that you come to the place where you can begin some of the deepest healing that you need.

I do not want to over-spiritualize health struggles. However, I want you to walk away understanding some pieces that you might need to address spiritually for health and healing. This will look different for everyone and it doesn't mean that there is some big spiritual stronghold that you need to break through for your healing to occur. Ultimately, you are in pursuit of wholeness, healing in every part of you, which means we need to address your spiritual health. It is when you can surrender to His loving will for your life and claim His promises of peace and healing that you will find your greatest freedom and joy, no matter your circumstances or health situation. Spend time with the Greatest Physician known to mankind. He knows your way, He knows how to heal, He knows your struggles and He knows perfect timing for you. He is always with you, He loves you and His desire for you is a truly abundant life because He *is* Life and Love.

Be prepared to be surprised and delighted by your deliverance and healing as you surrender it ALL – working through your identity, the emotional areas, physical areas, spiritual areas, past traumas and more. It *will* bring forth delightful fruit, freedom and joy because whole healing is His desire and promise to you. In fact, at this very moment, Jesus is singing His delight and healing over you because His heart is for you is love and His desire is for you to be a WHOLE, HEALED human being. <u>That is not an empty promise but a guarantee</u>. He takes what is broken and repairs the cracks, dents and chips. He takes what is sick and soothes, mends and heals. *His business is healing so your guarantee is healing. It might not look exactly like what you expected but it is guaranteed to be BEAUTIFUL because He only makes things that are beautiful.*

I'm beyond excited for you. The whole journey, the commitment to the holistic process is incredibly challenging at times but rewarding. You have Jesus on your side. Nothing can stand against you. I hope and pray that the above questions stimulated you to think about and pray about your spiritual life and your relationship with the God who made you and loves you. Spend some time with Jesus and share your heart – the disappointments, the griefs, the hopes, the lost dreams, the delays, the anger and your desires. Make this open and honest time with Him a regular discipline and your sanctum of rest and restoration. He deeply cares, He hears you and He answers you! Let the Great Physician tend to your soul wounds, physical hurts, emotional traumas and He will heal in His gentle, timely way.

Final Words

*He who began a good work in you will carry it
on to completion until the day of Christ Jesus.*
— Phil. 1:6

As you draw to the conclusion of this workbook, I want you to stop, pause and reflect on your journey over these past weeks, months or years. There is no judgment on how long it's taken to walk through this book. In fact, your healing is just beginning in some sense. You will continue to heal because your journey this side of heaven is about becoming more healed and whole, a reflection of our good and perfect Saviour Jesus. What a delight it is to know that you are promised abundant life *now* and you have the Holy Spirit guiding you and comforting you through the process.

I expect that you might come back to this book at times as you work through some other aspect of your healing or some new symptom pops up. This is normal and okay. Healing isn't linear and it often isn't instantaneous. Slow down. Practice the healing exercises. Do what you can day by day. And remember to take time to celebrate your healing as you move forward. Celebration is essential, powerful and its restorative. Lastly, take courage and do not fear! Your life and your health are in the hands of a loving heavenly Father who holds you secure, who is utterly, completely and wholeheartedly committed to you.

My hope is that you walk away from this book with a new perspective, a healed perspective on yourself and your health. Ultimately, my deepest prayer is that you have and will continue to encounter Jesus in new and refreshing ways. He knows your needs and your desires and He is more than capable of meeting them. He loves you more than you love yourself and wants the best for you more than you do! He is powerful, He is with you and He can do abundantly more than you can ask, think or imagine (Eph. 3:20). Find rest in His Presence because He is always present and faithful to be with you.

"May the God of hope fill you with all joy and peace as you trust in Him so that you may overflow with hope by the power of the Holy Spirit." – Rom. 15:13

Appendix A
Supplement Information & Discount Codes

Beef Organs
These can be purchased online through a Canadian retailer from **Nutrimal.co**
They carry beef liver pills or you can purchase a mix of beef organs called Organyze which contains kidney, spleen, liver, pancreas and heart.
Use code REVIVE for 20% off*[1]

Supplements – homeopathic, tinctures, etc.
Fullscript Dispensary
Fullscript is an online dispensary for natural health products. They carry many of the homeopathic products I have mentioned.
You can make an account at my store - **Revive Natural Health Dispensary** – and receive a 15% discount on all products.

Methylene Blue (MB)
MB can be purchased at **lifeblud.co** – it is labelled with a ? mark.
Use code REVIVE for a 10% discount*

Full Spectrum Light Bulbs
This online supplier carries a variety of light bulbs.
thehealthhome.shop
Code REVIVE saves you 10%*

---

[1] *I make a small percentage from the sale

Homeopathic Allergy Blends for Allergies
www.homeocan.ca carries Homeopathic blends – Allergy and/or Sinus

Adaptogens
One of my favourite blends is called Adrenasense which can be found in my favourites at my Fullscript store Revive Natural Health.

Earthrunner Sandals
Grounding sandals can be purchased through this link:
https://bit.ly/4d3nWuK
This is a US retailer so there will be a customs fee. They include this in their shipping costs.

Environmental Working Group
Ewg.org – look up EWG Dirty Dozen to find information on foods highest in pesticides. They also have information on body products and levels of toxicity.

Apps for download – Provide toxicity ratings!
Think Dirty, EWG Healthy Living, Good Guide, DetoxMe, and SkinSafe can be used to give info on the toxin rating and all you need to do is scan the barcode.

PEMF therapy
Therasage.com is a US based company that has a range of mats available that also have red light therapy and TENS therapy on the mat. I have the large mat and I love it! You can read more about the benefits of PEMF on their website.
Use code REVIVENH for 10% discount*

Red Light Therapy

lifeblud.co, a Canadian company has red lights for sale Use code REVIVE for 10% discount.*

Therasage.com is a US retailer of red light products. Use code REVIVENH for 10% discount.*

Mineral Supplements

Shilajit & Humic-Fulvic acid supplements can be purchased through Canadian retailer LeafSource. **buyleafsource.ca**

Appendix B
Nutrition Record

	Monday	Tuesday	Wednesday	Thursday	Friday	Saturday	Sunday
Breakfast							
Lunch							
Dinner							
Snack							

Appendix C
Activity Record

Day	
Sunday	
Saturday	
Friday	
Thursday	
Wednesday	
Tuesday	
Monday	

Appendix D
Symptoms Tracker

Symptom	Description	Time/Date

About the Author

Rachel Van Halteren is a Registered Nurse, Homeopathic Practitioner, Holistic Nutritionist and a lover of all things natural health. Her healthcare experience includes emergency nursing, nursing in remote northern First Nation's communities, teaching, coaching and running her own healthcare practice. She has also had opportunities to serve in medical missions in Latin America and Africa.

Teaching people about health is a passion of hers, particularly as it pertains to how they think about health and what it takes to truly heal at a deep level. Her desire is for people to gain a deeper understanding of how deeply connected mental, emotional, physical and spiritual health are and how healing in every area is necessary for true healing to occur. Having worked in both the allopathic and natural health world, her desire to help people navigate their healing journey in a more holistic way, benefiting from both systems.

She lives in Ontario, Canada where she gets to enjoy the beauty of Northern Ontario in the summer. She enjoys being in nature, lifting weights, baking, reading and learning.

You can find her online at www.revivenaturalhealth.com

Notes

[1] 2012 "Early eczema and the risk of childhood asthma: a prospective, population-based study" by Marit Saunes, Torbjørn Øien, Christian K Dotterud, Pål R Romundstad, Ola Storrø, Turid L Holmen, and Roar Johnsen (PMID: 23095804)

[2] Cojocaru, M., Cojocaru, I.M., & Silosi, I. (2010). Multiple autoimmune syndrome. *Maedica*, 5(2), 132-134.

[3] Negele, A., Kaufhold, J., Kallenbach, L., & Leuzinger-Bohleber, M. (2015). Childhood Trauma and Its Relation to Chronic Depression in Adulthood. *Depression research and treatment*, 2015, 650804. https://doi.org/10.1155/2015/650804

[4] Dhar, A.K., & Barton, D.A. (2016). Depression and the Link with Cardiovascular Disease. *Frontiers in psychiatry*, 7, 33. https://doi.org/10.3389/fpsyt.2016.0003

[5] Miller, A. H., & Binder, E. B. (2023). Guilt by Association: Inflammation and Shared Genetic Risk Between Stress-Related and Immune Disorders. *American Journal of Psychiatry*, 180(4), 259–261. https://doi.org/10.1176/appi.ajp.20230078

[6] Dube, S. R., Fairweather, D., Pearson, W. S., Felitti, V. J., Anda, R. F., & Croft, J. B. (2009). Cumulative childhood stress and autoimmune diseases in adults. *Psychosomatic medicine, 71*(2), 243–250. https://doi.org/10.1097/PSY.0b013e3181907888

[7] Yehuda, R., & Lehrner, A. (2018). Intergenerational transmission of trauma effects: putative role of epigenetic mechanisms. *World psychiatry: official journal of the World Psychiatric Association* (WPA), 17(3), 243-257. https://doi.org/10.1002?wps.20568

[8] Scorza, P., Duarte, C. S., Hipwell, A. E., Posner, J., Ortin, A., Canino, G., Monk, C., & Program Collaborators for Environmental influences on Child Health Outcomes (2019). Research Review: Intergenerational transmission of disadvantage: epigenetics and parents' childhoods as the first exposure. *Journal of child psychology and psychiatry, and allied disciplines*, *60*(2), 119–132. https://doi.org/10.1111/jcpp.12877

[9] Sangalang, C. C., & Vang, C. (2017). Intergenerational Trauma in Refugee Families: A Systematic Review. *Journal of immigrant and minority health*, *19*(3), 745–754. https://doi.org/10.1007/s10903-016-0499-7

[11] Bower, J. E., & Kuhlman, K. R. (2023). Psychoneuroimmunology: An Introduction to Immune-to-Brain Communication and Its Implications for Clinical Psychology. *Annual review of clinical psychology*, *19*, 331–359. https://doi.org/10.1146/annurev-clinpsy-080621-045153

www.ingramcontent.com/pod-product-compliance
Lightning Source LLC
Chambersburg PA
CBHW032223080426
42735CB00008B/683